Managing the Next Generation of Public Workers

Managing the Next Generation of Public Workers is a fresh and energetic look at the changing climate of diversity in the public and nonprofit workplace.

The workforce of the twenty-first century represents unparalleled complexity: Baby Boomers, GenX, GenY, and Millennials. Although that diversity may be challenging and often overwhelming for public managers, Madinah Hamidullah emphasizes the potential strengths that can be drawn from complex multigenerational relationships.

This handbook offers public and nonprofit managers the tools necessary to address generational differences and questions such as:

- How do the newer generations in the workplace differ on such fundamentals as work ethic, family values and retirement horizons?
- Are they recruited differently and do they expect a different mix of benefits—perhaps a better work-life balance as a tradeoff for a lower salary?
- How can diverse, generational perspectives in the workplace add value by questioning old, traditional assumptions?
- Will approaches to organizational decision making necessarily change as new generations take over?

The book is for public and nonprofit managers who recognize the challenges of managing a multigenerational workforce, and are therefore seeking helpful insights. This volume is a roadmap not only for human resource (HR) managers, but for all managers who must address the complexities of the human condition—complexities that are complicated by the most rapid succession of workforce generations that we have yet seen.

Madinah F. Hamidullah is an assistant professor and director of Undergraduate Programs in the School of Public Affairs and Administration at Rutgers University-Newark, USA. Her current research interests include diversity, generational differences, and public service motivation. She teaches courses in Public Management, Leadership, Human Resource Management and Service Learning. She received her PhD in Public Administration and Policy from the University of Georgia, USA.

MARC HOLZER, SERIES EDITOR

MUNICIPAL SHARED SERVICES
A Public Solutions Handbook
Alexander C. Henderson, Editor

E-GOVERNMENT AND WEBSITES
A Public Solutions Handbook
Aroon Manoharan, Editor

THE PUBLIC SOLUTIONS HANDBOOK SERIES

MARC HOLZER, SERIES EDITOR

Managing the Next Generation of Public Workers

A PUBLIC SOLUTIONS HANDBOOK

Madinah F. Hamidullah

Routledge
Taylor & Francis Group

NEW YORK AND LONDON

First published 2016
by Routledge
711 Third Avenue, New York, NY 10017

and by Routledge
2 Park Square, Milton Park, Abingdon, Oxon, OX14 4RN

Routledge is an imprint of the Taylor & Francis Group, an informa business

© 2016 Taylor & Francis

Library of Congress Control Number:
2015949954

ISBN: 978-0-7656-4748-1 (hbk)
ISBN: 978-0-7656-3739-0 (pbk)
ISBN: 978-1-315-71896-5 (ebk)

Typeset in Times
by Apex CoVantage, LLC

Printed and bound in the United States of America by
Edwards Brothers Malloy on sustainably sourced paper

Contents

Series Editor's Introduction

The impetus for this series of public management handbooks is simply that public managers must have ready access to the best practices and lessons learned. That knowledge base is surprisingly extensive and rich, including insights from rigorous academic studies, internal government reports and publications, and foundation-supported research. Access to that knowledge, however, is limited by substantial barriers: expensive books and academic journals; "thick" academic language and hard-to-decipher jargon; and the sheer volume of information available. Our objectives in initiating this series are to identify insights based in practice, build competencies from that knowledge base, deliver them at an affordable price point, and communicate that guidance in clear terms.

GROUNDED INSIGHTS

Each volume in the series will incorporate case-based research. Each will draw helpful insights and guidelines from academe, government, and foundation sources, focusing on an emerging opportunity or issue in the field. The initial volumes, for example, will address such timely issues as: Shared Services for Municipalities and Counties, E-Government and Websites, Managing Generational Differences, Public Sector Innovation, and Performance Measurement and Improvement.

COMPETENCIES

We are initiating this series of Public Solutions Handbooks to help build necessary competencies, empowering dedicated, busy public servants—many of whom have no formal training in the management processes of the public offices and agencies they have been selected to lead—to respond to emerging issues by delivering services that policy makers have promised to the public, carrying out their missions efficiently and effectively, and working in partnership with their stakeholders. Enabling practitioners to access and apply evidence-based insights will begin to restore trust in their governments through high-performing public, nonprofit, and contracting organizations.

Just as important, students in graduate degree programs, many of whom are already working in public and nonprofit organizations, are seeking succinct, pragmatic, grounded guidance that will help them succeed far into the future as they rise to positions of greater responsibility and leadership. This includes students in master of public administration (MPA), master of public policy (MPP), master of nonprofit management (MNPM), and even some master of business administration (MBA) and law (LLD) programs.

AFFORDABILITY

Handbook prices are often unrealistically high. The marketplace is not serving the full range of public managers who need guidance as to best practices. When faced with the need for creative solutions to cut budgets—educating for ethics, tapping the problem-solving expertise of managers and employees, or reporting progress clearly and transparently—a grasp of such practices is essential. Many handbooks are priced in the hundreds of dollars and are beyond the purchasing power of an individual or an agency. Journals are similarly priced out of the reach of practitioners. In contrast, each volume in the Public Solutions series will be modestly priced.

CLEAR WRITING

Although the practice of public administration and public management should be informed by published research, the books that are now marketed to practitioners and students in the field are often overly abstract and theoretical, failing to distill published research into clear and necessary applications. There is substantial, valuable literature in the academic journals, but necessarily written to standards that do not easily "connect" with practitioner audiences. Even in instances where practitioners receive peer-reviewed journals as a benefit of association membership, they clearly prefer magazines or newsletters in a straightforward journalistic style. Too often, they set the journals aside.

I am proud to announce the third in the Public Solutions Handbook series: *Managing the Next Generation of Public Workers*, authored by Madinah Hamidullah. The workforce of the twenty-first century represents unparalleled complexity: Baby Boomers, GenX, GenY, Millennials; and surely, other groupings will emerge. Although that diversity may be daunting and often overwhelming for public managers, Hamidullah emphasizes the potential strengths that can be drawn from complex multigenerational relationships.

This handbook offers public and nonprofit managers the tools necessary to address generational differences and related questions. How do the newer generations in the workplace differ on such fundamentals as work ethic, family values, and retirement horizons? Are they recruited differently, and do they expect a different mix of benefits—perhaps a better work-life balance as a trade-off for a lower salary? Are new generations likely to resemble Traditionalists and Baby Boomers as they mature, becoming less self-centered and more conscientious? Or will their personal priorities and behaviors necessitate more rigid organizational structures? How can diverse, generational perspectives in the workplace add value by questioning old, traditional assumptions? Will approaches to organizational decision making necessarily change as new generations take over?

This handbook is a strategic map for public and nonprofit managers who recognize the challenges of managing a multigenerational workforce and are therefore seeking helpful insights. This volume is a roadmap not only for human resource (HR) managers but also for all managers who must address the complexities of the human condition—complexities that are made more complex by the most rapid succession of workforce generations that we have yet seen.

Governments and nonprofits spend as much as 85 percent of their budget on human resources. Hamidullah's volume will help them make the most of those investments.

Marc Holzer
Editor-in-Chief, Public Solutions Handbook Series
Dean and Board of Governors Distinguished Professor
of Public Affairs and Administration
Rutgers, The State University of New Jersey–Campus at Newark

1

Introducing Generation Next

What's the big deal about the buzz on generations' characteristics (Baby Boomers, GenX, GenY, Millennials, etc.)? People have long worked with different groups in diverse and ever-changing workforces. Multigenerations are present in the workforce in greater numbers than ever before. Today, there are four generations operating in the workforce, and, just like managing any heterogeneous workforce, a better understanding of the similarities and differences may result in a more efficient and effective workforce. It is important to note from the beginning that when I speak of generations, I'm not just speaking about stereotypes. I'm speaking of *unique* characteristics that groups acquire due to their social upbringing. Times change, and the likelihood that someone born in the 1940s has the same experiences and societal exposure as someone born in the 1980s is very slim. If these two individuals have to work on the same team, it might be helpful to know what each brings to the table with respect to their generational outlook. Years of experience, education, technical skills, and work styles may not amount to anything if groups cannot work seamlessly together.

The purpose of this book is to help organizations recognize and adjust to the changing nature of the work environment. Multigenerations in the workplace present several challenges, but also opportunities for organizations to learn and grow. Any diverse work environment can be both a strength and a weakness, depending on how managers and employees choose to interact with one another.

PURPOSE OF THIS HANDBOOK

All generations have different personalities that explain their behavior in the workplace (Lancaster and Stillman 2002; Mitchell 2000). Some groups are more concerned with personal achievement; others may be more career-centric versus organization-centric. This handbook seeks to use academically based generational profiles as a typology. Popular and often outdated typologies have been used to describe individuals within organizations. For example, Downs (1967) suggested that a bureaucracy can be made up of zealots, advocates, statesmen, and climbers. Weber (1947) developed archetypes of leadership into phenotypes: the hero ("heroic charisma"), the father ("paternalistic

1

charisma"), the savior ("missionary charisma"), and the king ("majestic charisma"), each having their own influences on organizational dynamics. While bureaucrats, as referred to here, can take on many different personalities, generational research suggests that each cohort may have distinguishing characteristics.

Depending on the individuals who make up a specific generation, different groups of generations may have different behaviors in areas such as the length in which they stay in particular jobs based on, for example, their need for prestige. Older generations may remain in particular jobs longer as a function of the generational personality, because the generational perception is that job hopping is a negative quality. Yet younger generations may see job hopping as a necessary condition to achieving a particular status in their careers.

Within each generation, differences are often considered harsh stereotypes of cohorts of individuals (Lancaster and Stillman 2002; Mitchell 2000). While exploring these differences, however, it is important to note that the popular distinctions may or may not be useful tools to inform management practices. In order to learn about the distinctions that can benefit management teams and workforce agencies, this handbook seeks to explore the classifications of generational personalities to see if popular cultural explanations are valid and useful.

Public organizations at all levels of government have begun to plan human resource policies that take into account the differences that generations bring with them to the workforce (Young 2003). This volume contributes to the body of public administration and public management research by specifically evaluating the behavior of those generations in the workforce today. While exploring the question about whether generations differ in the ways they approach work, their interest in serving the public, and their time spent in jobs as well as organizations, we will examine generational characteristics and their possible influence on individual's career histories.

This handbook addresses a gap in the literature in a number of ways. Government has claimed that there will be a worker shortage based on the number of current eligible employees preparing for retirement (Boath and Smith 2004; Pynes 2002). At the same time, many government organizations have followed the private sector and have begun to put considerable resources and manpower into coming up with innovative ways to deal with generational cohorts in the workforce. The missing link here is any clear evidence showing that there are differences in how generations approach work. Simply put, are there social and historical influences that can change how different individuals will approach work?

Because generational literature suggests that social and historical events may change a cohort's perceptions toward particular organizations, one of the primary goals of this handbook is to explore the idea of younger cohorts who do not perceive government work as the trailblazing place of employment as have older generations. Additionally, drawing on public service motivation (Perry and Wise 1990; Brewer, Selden, and Facer 2000; Perry 1996, 1997), the handbook helps explain if (and why) older generational cohorts are more attracted to public sector work. If younger groups are not as attracted to public service work as their predecessors might be, the results could exacerbate the current trend of fewer younger workers choosing public service as their premier place of employment.

OUTLINE OF THE HANDBOOK

In addition to introducing and describing generational profiles, this handbook explores issues surrounding recruitment and retention of the next generation of workers. Chapter 2 discusses how different aspects of benefits and compensation play a role in generational work behavior. Chapter 3 provides guidance on volunteerism and civic engagement and generations. As future generations become more connected to public service and the notion of "giving back" to society, it becomes necessary to know how the workplace can help. Chapter 4 demonstrates how communication plays a part in the multigenerational workplace. Some workplace conflicts may simply be due to misunderstandings in formality or delivery of information. Mentoring, career development, and leadership succession—extremely pertinent issues to the next generation—are addressed in chapters 5 and 6. Managers may find that younger generations are eager to switch jobs and are anxious to be promoted. Included for managers are helpful tools to manage these expectations while retaining valuable employees. Chapters 7 and 8 talk about education and social networking as opportunities for organizations to become attractive employers and areas of interest for young workers. Organizations and schools must be able to properly market themselves to workers of *all* ages. Chapter 9 explores the changing landscape of public service motivation. If we once had professions where individuals were innately inclined to serve, such as hospitals and food banks, we must be prepared to anticipate shortages if that motivation is lacking in younger generations.

Finally, the handbook concludes by taking a look at what is next for younger workers and public service organizations. Individuals and organizational dynamics are constantly changing. Public service organizations must stay ahead of the curve to ensure that they have the best and the brightest working for them.

MANAGING GENERATIONS IN THE WORKPLACE

The problems presented by an aging workforce have led to increased attention to managing multiple generations in the workplace, partly as a means of effecting smooth transitions of responsibility from older and retiring workers to younger, less experienced workers. The public sector will be hit especially hard by aging and potential personnel shortages (Scott 2004), resulting in intense competition for talented employees. Managing multigenerations in the workforce is becoming an important topic of conversation in the contemporary public workforce, with policies relating to the rapidly changing and diverse makeup of its employees, including race, gender, sexual orientation, and religion. Due to the increased attention on these generational differences and the observations regarding the attitudes of the younger generation, personnel managers need to know of the substantive differences in how particular generations approach work.

Observers of popular culture (Lancaster and Stillman 2002; Mitchell 2000) contend that individuals belonging to different generational cohorts will approach work based on the social and historical conditions associated with their development. Some differences proposed by various human resource consultants suggest that younger generations are more likely to challenge authority, are less loyal to their organizations, and are looking for promotions based on performance rather than agreeing with promotions based on longevity (Smith 2007; Shelton and Shelton 2005). Additionally, researchers who focus on the public sector (e.g., Perry and Wise 1990; Perry 1996, 1997) have found that some individuals are predisposed to serving the public and therefore will be attracted to public sector work. Rarely observed in empirical study are social and historical factors that may influence an individual's desire to work for the public. As individuals grow and mature, they may develop different patterns toward work, which may influence the type of work they do and the kind of organization in which they choose to work.

Government agencies are seeing their workforces grow older and retire, and, at the same time, fewer people are going into the public service (Leibowitz 2004). The impending demands for suitable replacements for retiring public employees highlights the need for a better understanding of the motives of younger workers. Younger workers are the future of the workforce; understanding their values and motives will provide managers with the information needed to manage these younger workers.

Monetary constraints are often a major reason for government's lack of ability to attract and retain qualified personnel. The description of public employees created by politicians, civic leaders, voters, and clientele groups all affect the government's ability to be a competitive employer (Nigro and Nigro 2000), and civil service reform has tried to address the issue of image as a barrier to recruiting talented and qualified individuals into the public sector workforce. One example of such reform has taken place in Georgia with the implementation of "Georgia Gain." By removing traditional civil service protections, Georgia hopes to reward employees with a pay-for-performance system designed to motivate, reward, and retain high-quality public employees (Sanders 2004).

Recruitment and retention are top priorities for public organizations, and one way to address those issues is to examine the characteristics of individuals based on age, generational affiliation, and time with the organization so that the data can help assess where managers should concentrate their resources. Managers have the daunting task of organizing a large number of employees in an ever-changing workforce, so understanding how those individuals' age and life experiences affect their life and work can be beneficial in the larger process. Job behaviors that develop from individual maturation must be separated from those that are a result of the social and historical impacts that make up generational differences (if such differences exist), and plans that are being adopted to help offset the more traditional workforce trends in the public sector should be clear in defining what problems they are addressing. Moreover, the plans to respond to the trends that public employers are beginning to face can be improved greatly by looking more deeply into the differences between generations and, further, into how those differences can be managed in the workplace.

One significant example of the need to address generational trends lies in the transition of baby boomers out of the workforce. The baby boom generation comprises individuals who were born from 1946–1964; they make up approximately 30 percent of the state government workforces who were eligible to retire in 2005 (Scott 2004). The federal government faces a similar crisis; in the next three years, an additional 30 percent of federal workers will be eligible to retire (Liberto 2013). Fifty-three percent of federal civil servants and 71 percent of federal senior executives are eligible to retire (Leibowitz 2004). The average age of government employees ranges from 45 to 47 years old. This is higher than the average of the U.S. workforce, which is 42.3 (Lavigna and Flato 2014). In contrast, in 1999, 42 percent of state and local government employees were between the ages of 45 and 64 years old (Pynes 2002). As the workforce continues to age, employers must be aware of the irreplaceable knowledge, experience, and wisdom that will be lost when certain individuals leave the organization (Boath and Smith 2004).

By learning from members of the older generations who will be leaving the workforce, employers can create plans that collect the knowledge needed to maintain and then apply what does and does not work for managers and coworkers alike. A way for organizations to do this is to identify the knowledge that is most at risk and institutionalize it within career-development processes (Boath and Smith 2004). Additionally, organizations must build knowledge communities that capture expert as well as informal information and insights into how businesses operate and how information is transferred from one employee to the next. If businesses do not conduct these knowledge plans, organizational knowledge loss or "brain drain" can become a problem within the entire employment life cycle, including recruiting, hiring, performance, retention, and retirement (Boath and Smith 2004).

THE MAKING OF A GENERATION

Scholars define generations as recognizable groups of individuals who share a common history and significant life events at critical developmental stages (Lancaster and Stillman 2002). Generations also inform individual personalities by influencing their feelings toward authority and organizations, what work means to them, and how they attempt to satisfy specific desires (Kupperschmidt 2000). The most prevalent generations (see Table 1.1) in today's workforce are the Baby Boomers (Boomers) and Generation

Table 1.1

Mixing and Managing Four Generations of Employees

Generation Timeline			
1922–1945	1946–1964	1965–1980	1981–2000
Veterans, Silent, Traditionalists	Baby Boomers	Generation X, Gen X, Xers	Generation Y, Gen Y, Millennial, Echo Boomers

Source: Greg Hammill, "Mixing and Managing Four Generations of Employees," *FDU Magazine Online* (winter/spring 2005), www.fdu.edu/newspubs/magazine/05ws/generations.htm (accessed November 23, 2013).

X (Gen Xers), followed by Traditionalists and Millennials (Gen Yers) (Lancaster and Stillman 2002; Mitchell 2000).

Background on Generational Research

Generations collide in certain ways, and currently, because of longer life expectancies and postponed retirements, more generations are in the work place (Lancaster and Stillman 2002). With Millennials entering the workplace it will be the first time in history that four generations have been in the work place at the same time. The problem, or the challenge, is that each generation brings its own set of values, beliefs, life experiences, and attitudes to the workplace (see Table 1.2 and 1.3). In 1997, a company called Bridgeworks Corporation helped bridge the gap between generations by helping people in the workplace look beyond their own perspective to understand the events, conditions, values, and behaviors that make each generation unique. In 2000 and 2001, Bridgeworks conducted a nationwide survey of more than 400 individuals to help bring merit to the

---

Table 1.2

Personal and Lifestyle Characteristics by Generation

	Veterans (1922–1945)	Baby Boomers (1946–1964)	Generation X (1965–1980)	Generation Y (1981–2000)
Core Value	Respect for authority	Optimism	Skepticism	Realism
	Conformers	Involvement	Fun	Confidence
	Discipline		Informality	Extreme fun
				Social
Family	Traditional Nuclear	Disintegrating	Latch-key kids	Merged families
Education	A dream	A birthright	A way to get there	An incredible expense
Communication Media	Rotary phones	Touch-tone phones	Cell phones	Internet
	One-on-one	Call me anytime	Call me only at work	Picture phones
	Write a memo			E-mail
Dealing with Money	Put it away	Buy now, pay later	Cautious	Save, save, save
	Pay cash		Conservative	Earn to spend

Source: Greg Hammill, "Mixing and Managing Four Generations of Employees," *FDU Magazine Online* (winter/spring 2005), www.fdu.edu/newspubs/magazine/05ws/generations.htm (accessed November 23, 2013).

Table 1.3

Workplace Characteristics

	Veterans (1922–1945)	Baby Boomers (1946–1964)	Generation X (1965–1980)	Generation Y (1981–2000)
Work Ethic and Values	Hard work	Workaholics	Eliminate the task	What's next
	Respect authority	Work efficiently	Self-reliance	Multitasking
	Sacrifice	Crusading causes	Want structure and direction	Tenacity
	Duty before fun	Personal fulfillment	Skeptical	Entrepreneurial
	Adhere to rules	Desire quality		Tolerant
		Question authority		Goal oriented
Work is . . .	An obligation	An exciting adventure	A difficult challenge; A contract	A means to an end; Fulfillment
Leadership Style	Directive	Consensual	Everyone is the same	TBD*
	Command-and-control	Collegial	Challenge others	
			Ask why	
Interactive Style	Individual	Team player; Loves to have meetings	Entrepreneur	Participative
Communications	Formal; Memo	In person	Direct; Immediate	E-mail; Voice mail
Feedback and Rewards	No news is good news	Don't appreciate it	Sorry to interrupt, but how am I doing?	Whenever I want it, at the push of a button
	Satisfaction in a job well done	Money	Freedom is the best reward	Meaningful work
		Title recognition		
Messages that Motivate	Your experience is respected	You are valued	Do it your way	You will work with other bright, creative people
		You are needed	Forget the rules	
Work and Family Life	Ne'er the twain shall meet	No balance	Balance	Balance
		Work to live		

Source: Greg Hammill, "Mixing and Managing Four Generations of Employees," *FDU Magazine Online* (winter/spring 2005), www.fdu.edu/newspubs/magazine/05ws/generations.htm (accessed November 23, 2013).

*As this group has not spent much time in the workforce, this characteristic has yet to be determined.

idea that different generations may have different values and attitudes toward life that may be present in the workforce. One of the purposes of the survey was to demonstrate that ignoring such differences can lead to misunderstandings and a clash of the generations in the workplace (Lancaster and Stillman 2002).

The following profiles of generations are broad but were developed from survey research by the Bridgeworks Corporation (1997 and 2001). Each of the four generational cohorts is a typology that explains a group that shares a common history (Lancaster and Stillman 2002). These shared events and conditions determine who they are and how they see the world.

Traditionalists (born between the turn of the last century and the end of World War II, 1900–1945) are believed to prefer longtime careers with one company and to have strong beliefs in hard work and respect for leaders. The generational personality for this cohort is loyalty, which should suggest longer durations in each job since job changing carries a stigma for this cohort.

Baby Boomers (1946–1964) are considered the most competitive cohort of the generations, with almost 80 million peers this group has always had numbers against them when they entered the workforce. The term "Baby Boomers" comes from the boom in births from 1946 to 1964. As a generation affected by events such as the Vietnam War, civil rights, the Kennedy (JFK and Robert) and King assassinations, and Watergate, it seems only fitting that they would lack respect for and loyalty to authority and social institutions (Bradford 1993; Adams 2000; Kupperschmidt 2000). Boomers are currently feeling the crunch of simultaneously caring for aging parents and for their own children. Many are also working in positions of power in the workplace and carry with them the modest values of material success and traditional values (Miniter 1997; O'Bannon 2001). This group is motivated to make a change in the world, and they value money, titles, and recognition. The generational personality for this group is optimistic. But Baby Boomers are the least likely of all generations to report work as being their most important activity (Mitchell 2000). As we will see in chapter 3, Baby Boomers are similar to the younger generations in their holistic approach to work-life balance.

Generation X (1965–1980) is the generation of skepticism. While the Boomer generation is well known for its loyalty to collectivism, Gen Xers are often considered a product of financial, family, and societal insecurity (Jurkiewicz and Brown 1998), leading to a generation with a sense of individualism rather than collectivism. Based on their great diversity and a lack of solid traditions (Smola and Sutton 2002; Jurkiewicz and Brown 1998), which is often because they have witnessed their parents being laid off, Generation Xers are sometimes considered to be cynical and untrusting (Kupperschmidt 2000). As a generation that relies on team support, craves mentors, and values stable families, Gen Xers bring to the workplace practical approaches to problem solving (Karp, Sirias, and Arnold 1999; Jurkiewicz and Brown 1998; Kupperschmidt 2000; O'Bannon 2001). As a technically competent group that is most comfortable with diversity, change, and multitasking, they push for emphasis on similarities rather than differences (Kupperschmidt 2000; O'Bannon 2001). Gen Xers are often thought to ask, "WIFM?" [What's in it for me?] (Karp, Sirias, and Arnold 1999, 30). And they are expected to bring various values and attitudes to the traditional workplace, including a different approach to benefits and compensation, along with diverse ideas about work loyalty and commitment (Singer Group 1999). Changing jobs is seen as a necessary condition because Gen Xers have lost faith in institutions as a result of seeing and experiencing lots of businesses downsize and merge. Individuals in this cohort look for career security versus job security, suggesting a greater likelihood of having more jobs across a particular work history.

Generation Y (1981–1999) is the most recent addition to the workplace. We know very little about Gen Yers and the Millennials (those born 1981–present), due to the fact that both generations are just beginning to enter the workforce. Research suggests that if Millennials follow the lead of Gen Xers, they too will want higher salaries, more financial leverage, and flexible work arrangements (Jennings 2000; Smola and Sutton 2002). Millennials are connected to the world through technology 24 hours a day; they distrust institutions and voice their opinions (Ryan 2000; Smola and Sutton 2002). Due to the web-connected nature of this generation, Generation Y will probably be the first generation to be socially active since the 1960s and will have an abundant appetite for work. This realistic generation is classified as seeing job changing as a part of the daily work routine. Younger generations are more likely to have a "work to live" attitude versus the "live to work" attitude of their predecessors. This, however, does not mean that they do not value work; it is just more likely that they will seek out employment that will allow them to have the best work-life balance (Mitchell 2000).

Although the Bridgeworks corporation conducts research on survey data, it should be noted that this is a consulting firm with a product to sell. Their client lists include several public, private, and professional organizations. Many of their prescriptions are targeted toward the needs of public sector organizations. Whether individuals buy into this idea of generational differences, organizations like the American Management Association, International City/County Management Association (ICMA), International Public Management Association (IPMA-HR), Internal Revenue Service, and several universities have had presentations on how to manage generations in their workforce.

The technology revolution has exacerbated the possible clash between the generations, and the challenge in the modern workplace will be to figure out how to manage each generation appropriately. The costliness at the institutional level is an area for concern. Companies have established cultures and policies that may not fit with new employees entering the work world. Generational collisions at work can result in loss of valuable employees, reduced profitability, poor customer service, derailed careers, wasted human potential, and even health problems caused by stress (Lancaster and Stillman 2002).

When the different generational characteristics are applied to the development of civil service institutions, there may be "disconnects" when one generation tries to fit into an established system. The general idea is that a system set up by Traditionalists may not fit into the ideas and values of more recent generations. Traditionalists generally do not see "job hopping" as a desirable trait in employees. Many Generation X and Y members may see having multiple jobs as necessary to achieve desired salary and goals. Rules that were set up and seen by other generations as important safeguards at one time may now be seen as hindrances to efficient workflow processes. Generation X members are considered to be more focused on achieving a better work-life balance, whereas Generation Y members are simply more focused on self-gratification (Bowen 2000).

Due to the variance of the generations represented in the modern workforce—with oldest versus youngest having extremely diverse work ethics and expectations for themselves and the companies for which they work—there is much confusion as to how the public sector will be affected after the large number of employees who are from the older generations approach retirement. Some employers around the United States have begun creating plans to manage the upcoming generations in the workforce. Currently, organizations are able to observe some generations in the workplace for longer periods of time, which may explain the current obsession with generations in the workplace. What follows is a preview of some of the current initiatives being taken by employers to manage generations in the workplace.

RESPONSES TO MANAGING MULTIPLE GENERATIONS IN THE WORKFORCE

Government will be one of the first sectors to experience the consequences of an aging national workforce (Scott 2004). Some of the reasons for this phenomenon include the declining appeal of public service, competition with the private sector for talent, and lower retirement eligibility (Young 2003). This crisis may be mitigated by the economic downturn, eligible employees delaying retirement, and a renewed interest in public service after the attack of the World Trade Center in New York City on September 11, 2001, but public organizations are preparing themselves for managing an aging and retiring workforce. Public agencies have been urged to find strategic trouble spots by collecting necessary data to forecast the changing workforce.

Although governments on all levels (local, state, and federal) currently face several fiscal challenges, it is still important to prepare organizations for the changing composition of government. The Center for Organizational Research has encouraged public employers not to treat retirement as a "don't-ask-don't-tell" issue (Young 2003). Employees and employers should be able to discuss their retirement plans so that individual government agencies can assess where they may need to focus recruitment and retention. Recruitment and retention are of the utmost importance in keeping and screening for the best and brightest employees. Planning for retirement is directly related to current generational research due to the Baby Boomer generation approaching retirement age. Each generation will have a different relationship with the workplace as they develop in age. This relationship will have to be managed throughout the work life cycle of each employee.

Difference Between Age and Generation

We cannot ignore the connection between age and generational differences. The life cycle of stability concept (discussed further in chapter 5) suggests that generations really don't matter, but rather each generation will act a certain way based on when they are observed. In the life cycle of stability model, Traditionalists only appear to have preferences for long-term jobs because they are at a point in their lives where job hopping is not desirable. Because of these competing hypotheses, it is important to examine if there is any reason to continue giving attention to this notion of generational differences in the workplace.

Life course research is an area that is rarely studied in the field of public administration. Sociology and psychology often pull from work based in this area. Glen Elder is a leading researcher in life course theory, and his work emphasizes the value of linking life stages and examining transitions into research aging (Elder 1998). Life course research challenges researchers to look at aging as a continuing, lifelong process that can have turning points and starting and ending points, as well as a holistic impact on an individual's development (Elder and Johnson 2002).

The life-cycle approach to understanding aging suggests that individuals will have different values and experiences throughout the aging process. Young adults could be considered to have less stable values when compared to older adults (Johnson 2001). Booth, Francesconi, and Garcia-Serrano (1999) used the British Household Panel Survey and found that men and women held an average of five jobs over the course of their work lives, with half of these jobs occurring in the first ten years. Younger workers were found to have more separation hazards, which suggests that they may have an increase in job instability. As the number of jobs an individual held increased, the tenure in a particular job would lengthen (Booth, Francesconi, and Garcia-Serrano 1999). In the United States, the number of jobs held by men and women is nearly double the number held by British men and women (Booth, Francesconi, and Garcia-Serrano 1999; Hall 1982; Topel and Ward 1992).

Social psychology has informed much of the research on job values and the aging process, which suggests that job values and the rewards obtained on a job grow more important over time (Mortimer and Lorence 1979; Lindsay and Knox 1984; Kohn and Schooler 1983). Job tenure and job mobility are topics that need further exploration in public administration. In the case of U.S. federal employees, research has found that not only tenure but also an individual's dependence on the job, matter in the likelihood of quitting (Black, Moffitt, and Warner 1990). Based on work in this area, it is expected that older generational cohorts will have longer job durations than younger cohorts.

Caution should definitely be exercised when adapting policies and procedures geared toward generational differences. It seems that there is an age effect rather than a generational effect. There are no significant differences between the generations and job durations. The stigma of younger individuals job hopping may appear to be normal behavior for individuals early in their careers.

Previous studies have found that less experienced workers and those who feel poorly compensated for their jobs are more likely to leave (Mor Barak, Nissly, and Levin 2001). Organizations that invest in training and job-related education may help lessen the likelihood of individuals leaving their organization. The finding in the human services field suggests that individuals are not leaving their jobs for personal reasons, but more likely are leaving because they are not satisfied with their jobs, they feel excessive burnout, and they feel they are not supported by their supervisors.

MOVING FORWARD

This introduction summarizes the literature on multigenerations in the workplace and interest in public sector work. First, there are many public organizations adopting plans and investing resources to deal with generational differences in the workplace, with very little empirical evidence that these differences actually do exist and produce conflict in the work environment. People are working longer and may not retire when they become eligible. What may appear to be generational differences may be life stage differences.

Since recruitment and retention in the public sector are now of the utmost importance, public managers must understand the needs of the individuals they wish to employ. As public agencies and organizations try to develop new methods of recruitment and retention, younger generations will perhaps prefer different items in a benefits package. Younger generations are described as trying to find a better work-life balance, so compressed work schedules, job sharing, and telecommuting might be things that public agencies may adopt in response to employee demand. Baby Boomers are also expected to approach retirement in a different way than the generations before them (Singer Group 1999). Not only are Baby Boomers working longer, but they may also favor different retirement options like phased retirement or part-time employment. Generation X may not be different from those who came before them based on shared experiences, but rather the current life stage that those individuals are in may make some jobs more attractive than others.

Generational differences and their possible impacts on public management and personnel policies have and will remain a hot topic of debate in both popular literature and human resource management. Ultimately, generational differences will continue to be discussed because the prevalence of multiple generations will be visible in and outside the workplace for the foreseeable future. If generations do indeed differ, managers living twenty-five years apart should have different work values and be attracted to different aspects of work. The argument that generational researchers are making suggests that work values will be influenced by life events and socialization more than by age and maturity. It seems commonplace for one generation to complain about the work ethic or behaviors of the generations that follow. The obvious questions are: If each subsequent generation is in fact lazy or self-centered, do individuals become more conscientious and less self-centered with maturity (Smola and Sutton 2002)? Do previous generations forget how they used to be when they were young and stereotype younger generations for going through a natural stage in development?

This handbook will provide managers and employees at all levels of public and nonprofit organizations with the tools necessary to manage generational differences in the workplace. Generational differences may often be overlooked because they can intersect with other diversity aspects in the workplace. Race, gender, socioeconomic status, and age all play a part in the makeup of an individual's personality and work attitudes. This handbook will help highlight those differences that can be attributed to generational differences and further discuss how they can be overcome in the workplace. Just like any aspect of diversity, generational differences should be seen as an added benefit to the workforce. Managers can benefit from the diversity of thought and opinions that generational differences provide. If growing up in a particular time shapes a person's attitude, it could also shape a person's decision-making approach. If people of all generations are providing input on addressing issues facing the public at large, the overall decision making process could be improved. Generational differences can result in conflict or compromise in the public workplace. This handbook will provide the guidance necessary to ensure that an awareness of differences adds value to public and nonprofit workplaces.

2

The Future Workplace

Recruitment, Retention, Benefits, and Compensation

RECRUITMENT AND RETENTION OF GENERATION NEXT

As we begin to explore generational differences, it is important not to treat any generational profiles simply as stereotypes. Generational profiles are descriptions of the average member in a particular generational profile (Twenge and Campbell 2008). Have a job, post a job description, interview applicants; fill the position. . . . It's that easy, right? Recruitment and retention in the future may not be so simple and certainly not as straightforward as in the past. This is due not only to the differences in the generations but also the changing climate of hiring and retaining workers.

The General Services Administration (GSA) reports a high demand for entry-level jobs, but mid- to upper-level jobs are really where recruitment is becoming more difficult (Losey 2013). This presents a situation where paying attention to current generational trends might be helpful. Why are organizations not seeing solid steps of succession with employees? If there are current challenges in filling leadership positions, what can organizations do to make the cycle stop? Getting good employees in the door is just the beginning. Having an organization that has the ability to *retain* top talent is what leaders should strive to see.

Government Morale and Appearance

Attraction to government work is an ongoing challenge for organizations. Government furloughs, shutdowns, and sequesters do not help make government work an attractive option to prospective employees, both young and old (Losey 2013). The constant public message and perception that something is wrong with public service makes it harder for organizations to recruit young talent (Losey 2013). Once those individuals are in the organization, they need to be retained.

Employee Commitment

In addition to regular life-cycle job movement, younger generations see job change as a normal part of seeking career success. Organizations can boost employee loyalty by providing opportunities to learn new skills, challenging jobs, higher compensation or benefits, and greater opportunities for advancement and promotion (Tolbize 2008). Younger generations are especially interested in being associated with organizations that are founded on values. Younger generations are known for being in search of happiness and working for organizations that they feel align with their values. This could benefit both employee and employer. Younger generations do not see jobs as just a place to go and collect a paycheck. They will strive to have a job that fulfills them not just financially but personally as well. This is a different approach to work than that of the Traditionalists and Baby Boomers, for whom jobs signify a means to an end, a point of pride and status, and a means of providing for nuclear families.

Respect and Authority

Both younger and older workers seek respect and attention in the workplace. The need for authority is found to vary among generations. Deal (2007) found that Traditionalists had a greater respect for authority when compared to other generations and considered it one of their top values. The style of leadership that is preferred by older generations is more aligned with the command and control structures you would see in the military. Younger generations, especially Xers and Yers, are more comfortable with authority and do not see superiors as intimidating (Deal 2007). Questioning authority is common with younger employees, and this should not always be seen as a sign of disrespect. Younger generations, with their more collaborative nature, do not see superiors as untouchable characters even if they are working in a top-down oriented organization. All generations seek respect and want to be listened to, heard, and valued. However, older generations may believe they are not respected in the workplace. They desire respect for their experience, and this could present a challenge for managers trying to establish a standard for respect across all generational lines. Younger workers require clear instructions, and they will resist micromanagement and need space to complete their assigned tasks (Joyner 2000).

RECRUITMENT AND RETENTION AND LESSONS FROM OTHER FIELDS

When recruiting younger generations, organizations may have to use nontraditional methods such as social media (Twitter, Facebook, LinkedIn, etc.). Younger generations rely more on technology than previous generations do. As the future workforce changes, organizations may have to change as well. Employers in the public healthcare field are experiencing shortages in employees, and, as a result, they pay more attention to recruitment and retention efforts. Individuals being unable to retire due to the recession of 2008 may have temporarily saved some industries from the lasting effects of workplace shortages. In several industries, new college graduates are having difficulty finding work because older employees did not retire as expected. Graduates will be seeking careers where they find the most promising job prospects.

Retaining all generations of workers can be helpful for organizations. Workers are most likely to stay at organizations that make them feel valued (Smola and Sutton 2002). It may be necessary to hold on to older generations to ensure proper transitions of new workers. Organizations should ensure that they do not lose valuable information and knowledge when older workers leave the organizations. Having solid succession plans and engendering younger generations who can see their future with an organization will be the key to retaining younger workers. Younger generations may be seen as less committed to their jobs, but they will be more entrepreneurial in their careers than previous generations. They will likely not join organizations expecting long-term employment. They will always be free agents because the employee-employer bond is no longer intact.

In 1974 and 1999 studies that compared Baby Boomers and Generation Xers and their respective work values, it was found that older workers have lower desires for promotion (Smola and Sutton 2002). This could mean that different generations may make better pairings in the workplace. Baby Boomers—because of their curiosity, goal orientation, and loyalty—are closer in work qualities to Traditionalist and make a better pairing (Hammill 2005). Groups can always learn from one another, so separation is not the key. Younger workers need to learn the organization, and it may be best to set up mentoring networks that cross generational lines. As with anything that makes individuals different from each other, it may be that those very differences present the biggest assets for the organization and the employee.

Good business is based on the understanding of the differences that exist among us. This will not just be limited to generations but will also involve larger issues of diversity than exist within our current workforce and society. Managing this kind of diversity should not be taken lightly and should be a focus of top leaders and human resource departments. Human capital is an important resource, and the management of this resource should be as important as managing time, money, and building space. We all work harder for organizations that are productive, efficient, effective, and high-quality. Managing the varying generations will be an important part of achieving any kind of diversity maintenance. Public administrators can learn from other industries when dealing with issues of recruitment and retention. While they may not be suffering from a complete lack of employees, an organization's professional associations can be a great way to keep individuals engaged with the profession. An individual's commitment to the purpose and action will determine his or her decisions to join and stay with work-related organizations. Generational differences influence membership in a number of ways. Younger professionals may not see the benefit of joining professional organizations. One way organizations can start recruiting younger members is to encourage the use of university students and have student run chapters. With Baby Boomers postponing retirement, many younger workers find it hard to find employment. This is just the beginning of a larger issue. Eventually, Boomers will retire, and those vacancies that were expected years ago will suddenly open up. Managers need to ensure that they have a direct channel to prospective employees. Employment internship programs with local colleges and universities can provide opportunities for organizations to ensure that their employees with prior organizational knowledge can connect with younger potential employees. These programs can be formal or informal. Formal programs may guarantee a constant supply of students who can help bridge the gap between theoretical school work and practical application of knowledge.

Beyond internship programs, mentoring programs can help with recruitment and retention. Once they are in an organization, individuals want to know how their careers can progress. Programs that let employees know they have a future at their place of employment can help with retention. Younger employees are often impatient when it comes to job promotions and advancing their careers. A program outlining expectations and opportunities helps ease feelings of uncertainty, and career programs and management within organizations can help employees of any level.

Maintaining the right workforce is essential to organizational success. One way organizations can ensure the success of their workforce is by making themselves more attractive to a new generation of workers. This may include moving traditional recruiting techniques from organizational websites to social media. Facebook, Twitter, and LinkedIn are all valuable resources that organizations can use to help them enhance recruitment outreach. Young and old employees alike are looking to the Internet and social networking websites for employment opportunities. Human resource departments should be sure they are taking advantage of these valuable resources.

Younger generations seek and crave feedback. A possible retention technique can be regular employee evaluations (Jarousse 2011). Yearly evaluations may not provide enough information for some employees. While it may be time consuming to provide thirty- or ninety-day evaluations, turnover is a costly matter, and retaining qualified employees is worth it. Regular evaluations can provide valuable feedback and act as "course corrections" for employees who are not in line with organizational expectations. Formal and informal evaluation processes can be useful retention tools when it comes to both new and old employees (see chapter 4 on generational communication). For younger employees, evaluations and reward/recognition programs can be ways to show support. A small amount of recognition can provide a large amount of satisfaction for employees. Recognition and reward programs can help after formal evaluations, but "mini" programs can also be used between evaluations. Focusing on retention is something for managers of all generations to take seriously. From Traditionalists to Millennials, each group will have needs and important desires.

We want to protect public organizations from facing a unique talent crisis. Although we are facing a surplus in job seekers, many organizations have shortages in workers because they need workers with critical, high-level skills (Erickson, Schwartz, and Ensell 2012). Organizations should not assume that high unemployment, equates to a large number of qualified individuals in their particular sector. This talent paradox will put public organizations in competition with nonprofit and for-profit organizations for employees with highly specialized skills. Focusing on retention of the most skilled employees helps to navigate the talent paradox. Jobs that individuals took during the recession or 2008 may not be long-term options for employees. Younger employees who just joined the job market may have been forced to find employment in organizations that had openings; when better organizations begin hiring again, those employees may take the opportunity to leave. Employment choice is highly correlated to the other job opportunities that exist in the market.

Organizations should take an inventory of skills to determine which are most important to them and should invest in learning how these skills may change across industry and generational levels. Different groups want different things, and personalized approaches to recruitment and retention may be a necessary evolution of human resource management. After identifying critical skills, the next step is to find out what individuals desire. Taking surveys to gauge employees' needs can help organizations determine if they are providing the right employment packages for their workers. Human resources departments should not assume that they are providing the correct employment benefit packages or that they know employees' needs. These needs will change constantly, and staying up-to-date will be key to retaining the skills needed for the organizations. When recovering from the depression of 2008, Millennials and Generation Xers will likely look for promotions and financial incentives, while Baby Boomers will be looking for recognition (Erickson, Schwartz, Ensell 2012). Millennials want companies that are responsible and care about volunteerism, while Generation Xers are more concerned with work-life balance. Having different approaches to employee retention will be necessary for the changing culture of work. Technology, culture, and the economy all influence employees' decisions to stay with their places of employment. Managing the catalysts for high turnover rates is important before an organization reaches a critical need for employees. Organizations must take an aggressive approach to branding themselves and understanding how this affects their employees. The talent paradox is not something organizations should take for granted. A worker surplus does not mean that there will be workers with the knowledge, skills, and abilities needed in the organization.

GENERATIONAL DIFFERENCES FOR BENEFITS AND WORK VALUES

Most of the debate about multigenerations in the workplace centers on the difference in the life stage development. One set of principles, the Protestant work ethic, dates back to the sixteenth century and is described as a belief that hard work, dedication, frugality, and perseverance are both pleasing to God and necessary for salvation (Steiner and Steiner 2000). While similar work values are prevalent elsewhere and at other times, it is not surprising that a common definition of work values is elusive. As with any value, work values help to define what people believe is right and wrong (Smola and Sutton 2002). Since the workplace is not a place that can be separated into right and wrong, it is important that current work values align with current work conditions. Modern work environments require decision making, problem solving, troubleshooting, and, often, the managing of difficult situations. Due to this, work values could be defined as a structural framework that reflects the central elements of the construct and reduces confusion over its conceptual boundaries (Dose 1997). More recently, Smola and Sutton (2002) defined work values as follows: "Work values are the evaluative standards relating to work or the environment by which individuals discern what is right or assess the importance of preferences." To really explore generational differences, attention must be paid to the changing nature of work as well as individuals' view of work.

The Singer Group is an organizational consulting firm that gives a popular description of current generations in the workforce in an effort to help businesses manage people and their organizations. The term "free agents" often categorizes the retention of Gen Xers. Flexible work schedules alongside consulting work and temporary work are often valued by this younger generation (Singer Group 1999). When being compensated, Gen Xers are often categorized as "independent contractors" with a need for rapid results and broader roles rather than specialized jobs (Singer Group 1999). Attitudes toward retirement include "pay me now and I'll take care of myself," and Xers often do not see social security retirement benefits as something they will receive (Singer Group 1999). Overall, workplace policies for Gen Xers include work flexibility and work-life balance; they will not sacrifice personal or family-related goals for their careers (Scanlon and Pitt-Catsouphes 2005).

The Catalyst organization (2005) explored some additional assumptions about Generation Xers. Because this generation was one of the first to see both of their parents working long hours, corporate downsizing, and the collapse of several corporations, it could be expected that they might approach work and careers differently. A study of more than 1,200 working professionals found that Gen Xers did not have low levels of work commitment. Of the Gen Xers surveyed, 85 percent said they really care about the fate of their employers (Catalyst 2005). Gen Xers value career development and advancement.

Recent scholarship on generational differences found that work values differ among generations and change as workers age (Smola and Sutton 2002). In a survey of 350 U.S. workers (mentioned earlier in this chapter), Smola and Sutton compared the 1999 and 1974 survey results to try and understand if an individual's work values are influenced more by generational experiences, or if they change over time with age and maturity. Regardless of generational affiliation, it was found that American workers are trying harder to balance work and personal goals (Smola and Sutton 2002). It is important for Generation X employees to feel valued by their employer. If turnover is too high among Baby Boomers, Traditionalists, or Generation Xers, then knowledge will be lost on every level of the organization.

Trying to separate the connection between how individuals age and mature from how history affects growth is not something easily done. The causal link between how history and maturation affect an individual is often unclear and, at times, interdependent. Separating the causal connection and causal explanation can be difficult and presents a challenge for researchers dealing with history and maturation (Cook and Campbell 1979; Cook 1993). The direct cause and effect of generational differences for work differences among generational cohorts is challenging to link because of the maturation effects of each group. There are two causes for this difference: historical/social effects and maturation that are in play and will have an effect on each generational cohort. Recognizing that this is a challenge, one goal of this handbook is to explore the challenge empirically using statistical techniques.

There have been various attempts to separate individuals' changing work values that are associated with aging from those that can be associated with generational experiences. As individuals age and mature, their relationship with and understanding of work may change. Generational scholars believe that this relationship with work will also have unique periods due to generational affiliations. Student values have been found to change from middle school, to high school, to college, and to the workforce (Walsh, Vacha-Haase, and Kapes 1996). Singer and Abramsom (1973) found no change in worker values over a twelve-year period, while Rhodes (1983) found that work attitudes, values, and satisfaction change when workers pass through particular career stages (not life stages).

Popular culture has done a good job talking about generational differences in every aspect of society. Generational categories are neat, generalizable ways to look at individuals. These differences should be fully explored before managers try to incorporate them into their policy design. This handbook looks at some of the popular stereotypes of generational cohorts to see if they are worth the time and the consideration they are receiving. Many techniques and policies can be used to help manage generations and workforces that have increased diversity of any kind.

One recruitment technique employers can use to help manage a generationally diverse workforce is to provide a competitive benefits package. Benefits can make or break an individual's decision to join a particular organization. At a time when pay may not be the main attraction, childcare, flexible schedules, and other select benefits can help recruit employees into the organization. For Millennials, think about *Charlie and the Chocolate Factory*. The character Veruca Salt is a spoiled rich girl who wants a golden ticket. She goes on to sing a song about not caring how she gets her golden ticket, but she "wants it now." That is the attitude held by the newest generation in the workplace, GenY. They want rewards, praise, feedback and attention. Now. This does not mean they are annoying or inconsiderate of their managers' time, but they grew up in a time where feedback was instant, and, thanks to technology, that is what they expect. Also called the "microwave generation," they are accustomed to having things immediately, and, because of the technology they were raised on, instant results are commonplace. Managers may have to adapt to the needs of these workers. Not receiving immediate feedback may make younger workers feel unappreciated and undervalued. This in turn could lead to unnecessary turnover. One form of feedback for younger workers could be as simple as hearing, "job well done!" For older generations money and job security was the only feedback they needed.

WORK–LIFE BALANCE

Younger generations saw their parents lose jobs and careers even after sacrifices were made at the expense of their families and personal relationships (Kersten 2002). These individuals are going to be less likely to let work interfere with other parts of their lives (Tolbize 2008). Younger generations of workers are perceived to have higher levels of narcissism, which results in higher levels of performance expectations in the workplace.

Workers with higher levels of self-esteem want work that places them in positions of influence (Twenge and Campbell 2008). Many of these desires are going to be expected immediately upon joining an organization. Managing expectations of workers of all ages is going to be critical for organizations.

Younger workers are a new breed of employees that will seek, demand, and expect fulfillment and meaning from their work (Twenge and Campbell 2008). This is different from Boomers and Traditionalists. Younger workers will be more likely to walk away from jobs when they do not find meaning and purpose in their work. Where economic factors may prevent all workers from exercising the option to leave, younger employees will seek fulfilling and authentic work. Job satisfaction, commitment, and performance can be influenced by the employee's understanding of the employer's expectations. Younger employees expect the employee-employer contract they were promised when hired, so if the actual work does not match their expectations, they may become disenchanted with their jobs (Robinson and Morrison 2000). One way that organizations can combat the inconsistencies of expectations is to have employees draft their expectations of the position and discuss it with them often. One thing most employees know is that written job descriptions rarely match the tasks that happen once they begin a job. Younger employees will expect direct correlations, and when there are changes, their ability to adjust is not as established as older generations. Feedback and regular checkups will enhance the employee's connection to the organization and allow for any inconsistencies in employment expectations to be discussed.

Evaluation of younger employees may become more time consuming but effective when trying to retain promising young workers. Self-evaluations may not be as effective with a generation that possesses higher levels of narcissism. These same workers may not respond well to the "360 evaluations" of the past. One-on-one feedback and assessment from mangers will be a successful tool for the evaluation of younger workers.

TELECOMMUTING

The term telecommuting—first coined by Nilles (1975) and also known as telework—was originally seen as a solution to many social and organizational challenges. Organizations are supposed to be able to reduce real estate costs, help employees balance work-life challenges, and achieve compliance with the Americans with Disabilities Act of 1990 (Bailey and Kurland 2002). Along with contributing to environmental factors like less traffic congestion and air pollution reduction, telecommuting can be an overall win for employees, employers, and the larger community. But, even as telecommuting first started taking hold, very little was known about its effectiveness. As a response to a more technology-based society, telecommuting allows employees to work outside the traditional workplace.

Many large private organizations are ending the telecommuting trend within their organizations. In February and March of 2013, Yahoo and Best Buy (respectively) began to reevaluate their telecommuting policies. Many government organizations may find the need to reevaluate such workflow processes. One of the factors organizations are starting to see is the need for face-to-face interaction and the positive benefits that stem from those interactions. Telecommuting has also been associated with the loss of traditional workplace benefits and corporate affiliation (Bailey and Kurland 2002). So, it is important for managers to understand the true nature of telecommuting and the impact it can have on the organization at large.

It is an even more important time for employers to establish a legitimate connection with employees, and readdressing workplace processes just might be an area where this can happen. Managers could require workers to work in the office for the beginning of their employment term to ensure that they are acclimated to the organization prior to beginning a telecommuting schedule. Organizations are using in-office workers as a way to set clear expectations. One way that human resources departments can help is by setting clear guidelines for teleworkers. This may be an attractive option for workers of all generations. Baby Boomers often find themselves caring for parents and children, and having flexible work schedules may help them balance these competing demands. New work arrangements should not just be seen as a recruitment tool for new workers. It also can be used as a retention tool for current workers. Taking stock of what employees want is something organizations cannot ignore.

Outcomes that organizations look for from telecommuters not only include improved productivity but also job satisfaction (Bailey and Kurland 2002). Little empirical evidence is available to support the higher job satisfaction claim because it is often difficult to get telecommuters to participate in such studies. And, the varied nature of teleworkers is hard to judge as well. Does someone who works from home once a week consider himself or herself a telecommuter like someone who only has a virtual office space? Another idea is limiting titles and classifications to reduce the hierarchy of jobs. If flexible schedules are offered to some workers, it might be in the best interest of managers to offer them to everyone in that particular worker classification. Doing so can limit the appearance of unfair practices and favoritism. Employers may also allow certain workers to try flexible schedules to see if it is an arrangement that works for them. This allows employees to have a greater appreciation for their current schedule and arrangements. Employers also need to define what qualifies for telework. It may not be the solution to all problems, and, as many private sector organizations have learned, bringing work back into the office may be the solution for the future. Public and nonprofit organizations often follow the private sector when it comes to staffing and workplace trends, so it must be a policy that is monitored, especially in how it applies to multigenerations.

POINTS TO REMEMBER

- Internship programs can be a useful tool: these programs can help with recruitment efforts and also give students short-term exposure to organizational operating procedures.
- Survey employees to gauge how an organization is doing before it is too late. Turnover is costly to any organization, and if there are systematic reasons for employees leaving, they should be addressed.

- Retention reasons may differ across generations: know what is keeping employees happy and satisfied with the organization.
- Regardless of generation, individuals at different life stages will have different needs, and these will need to be addressed throughout an individual's tenure with an organization.
- Provide à la carte benefit packages; customizable packages will be attractive to younger generations who are getting married and buying homes later in life. Benefits like gym memberships, transportation credits, and selective healthcare may be better suited for some employees.
- Pay close to attention to younger generations and their need for greater work-life balance.
- Understand employee motivation: what makes employees engage and believe in an organization will contribute to the overall organization efficiency within any organization.

3

Volunteering

A SPECIAL RELATIONSHIP: BABY BOOMERS AND MILLENNIALS

Social and civic engagement can take on many different forms. Volunteering, mentoring students, donating money, giving resources, establishing community gardens, and building homes are just a few ways individuals can give back to their communities. Reasons for giving back depend on many variables, including generational differences. Organizations knowing their particular needs for volunteers can better tailor their recruitment efforts to certain groups. A projected increase in volunteer rates among adults should be encouraging for nonprofit organizations, and organizations should to be ready to capitalize on those possibilities.

Teenage volunteering rates are generally considered "episodic" (ninety-nine or fewer hours per year) and are most likely to be served with educational or youth service organizations (Reingold and Nesbit 2006). Organizations that are more likely to attract young workers generally have special days of service that can give individuals exposure to the organization. One good predictor of volunteering is prior service or relationship with the organization so any start is better than never getting individuals involved. Teenagers are most likely to volunteer with educational organizations, youth service organizations, social organizations, and community organizations.

Baby Boomers make up the largest groups (nearly 75 percent) of those volunteering in the United States (Reingold and Nesbit 2006). This group is more likely to volunteer with religious organizations than are quarter-life adults or older teenagers. Volunteering rates for older adults has been increasing over the last three decades—from 14.3 percent in 1974 to 23.5 percent in 2005 (Reingold and Nesbit 2006). This is informative as life-cycle events may trigger an individual's decision to begin giving back to their communities or other organizations of choice. Episodic volunteering has increased among all ages including Boomers. The difference, however, is that Boomers generally do not limit their volunteering to one organization; they may spread their hours out over multiple organizations. Baby Boomers are most likely to volunteer with educational, religious, and youth services.

All generations are shaped and bonded because of the life events they have experienced at particular ages (See Table 3.1). Generation Xers and Millennials will be largely

Table 3.1

Generational Differences and Common Attributes

The following is a closer look at the main distinctions between Boomers, Gen Xers and Millennials.

	Baby Boomers (1946–1965)	Gen Xers (1966–1978)	Millennials (1979–2001)
Characteristics	The "me" generation • Narcissistic • Intellectual renaissance • Judgmental	Disillusioned cynics • Cautious and skeptical • Searching for self • Alienated and confrontational • Alternative	Optimistic and confident achievers • Disciplined and accepting of authority • Well-educated and competitive • Upbeat and open-minded • Entitled
	Baby Boomers came of age post–World War II, at the height of an intellectual reawakening in America. As youths, Boomers rebelled against the Establishment and the over idealized, team-oriented generations that came before them.	As a group, Gen Xers are a product of a strongly individualistic society. Thought of as a generation of slackers with little drive and no direction, Gen Xers are antirules and antigroups. They rely on self over others.	Reared in a youth-centric culture, Millennials are self-assured and civic-minded. With sophisticated social awareness, Millennials believe community extends beyond their own backyard, and feel empowered and compelled to make the world a better place.
Defining Experiences	• Summer of Love • Civil Rights • Vietnam War • Sexual Revolution	• AIDS • Recession • Soaring divorce rates	• Digital age • Terrorism and natural disasters • A global economy
	Social change and political push-back marks the Baby Boomer era. Boomers fought against race and gender inequality, participated in antiwar protests, and supported sexual freedom, all within the refuge of an affluent America. This highly politicized generation was intent on challenging the status quo.	Gen Xers were faced with a social climate in the midst of advancements in medicine and technology, the War on Drugs, an unknown and deadly disease, times of recession, and the splintering of the American family. Collectively, Gen Xers were not considered capable of rallying together to improve the state of the world.	Millennials have grown up in an environment where technology provides a platform for customization and immediate gratification in all aspects of life. News and information travel freely across continents, with recent acts of terrorism and natural disasters touching more than the people directly involved. As a result, Millennials have been instilled with a far-reaching, global social conscience.

(Continued)

Table 3.1

(Continued)

	Baby Boomers (1946–1965)	Gen Xers (1966–1978)	Millennials (1979–2001)
The State of the Family	• Pampered children of stay-at-home moms • Defined gender roles • Affluent, stable families As children, Boomers were indulged by their parents and grew up in households with clear and separate gender roles destined to be torn down and redefined. As parents, Boomers' primary focus is on "self" (i.e. self-improvement), which inherently positions the needs of the family unit in second place.	• Children of divorce • Latchkey kids • Loose adult supervision • Family as a source of conflict Gen Xers experienced their childhood in an adult-centric society where parents practiced "hands off" parenting and were not always around. Gen Xer parents tended to concentrate on their own happiness rather than focus on their Gen X child's successes and/or disappointments.	• Highly-involved parents • Strong family bonds • Nurtured at home • Family as a source of support Millennials came of age in a child-centric society. Both the increase in fertility treatments and rise of youth advocacy in politics has helped establish that Millennial children are valued and protected. The generation gap has all but disappeared, as parents and children understand one another and have more in common than ever before.
Personal Measures of Success	• Long-term employment • Job titles and promotions • Self-actualization	• Flexible work times • Jobs on their terms • Healthy and stable relationships	• Personal fulfillment at work • Active lives outside of work • Healthy and strong community

Common Attributes for Each Age Segment

Teens	College-Aged	Young Adults
• Burgeoning independence • Full parental support • Friends are strong influence • Beginning to find their own identity	• First time on their own, but parents still very involved • Friends are everything • Shaping and defining their identity • Expect to succeed now and in the future (postcollege)	• Independent, but parents are still there to back them up • Taking on adult responsibilities (family and financial) • High achievers, team players in their professional world • Value having a satisfying life outside of work

Source: Cone Inc., and AMP Agency, *The 2006 Cone Millennial Cause Study—The Millennial Generation: Pro-Social and Empowered to Change the World* (Boston: Cone Communications), 4, 5, www.prnewsonline.com/Assets/File/ConeMillennialCauseStudy_2006.pdf.

influenced by events like September 11, 2001, and the Boston Marathon bombing in 2013. Witnessing such events helps bolster their interest to serve and give back to the community. Other events like natural disasters (both domestic and abroad) increase volunteering. Not only are younger generations more likely to be affected by events in the United States at a young age, but, because of the rapid access to information, they will also be aware of international disasters and may feel a calling to respond to those causes.

As the number of nonprofit organizations increases, so do the number of volunteering opportunities for everyone. The demand for volunteers also increases as a result. An increase in the number of nonprofits will also increase the likelihood that individuals will find an organization that relates to their causes. Variety can be a good and bad thing for organizations because it also increases the need for better volunteer management. Groups that become reliant on volunteers to sustain program delivery need to ensure that they have a solid roster of volunteers. Nonprofit organizations can rely on professional staff only up to a certain point.

Baby Boomers and Millennials are both very special generations when compared to other generations. Their size sets them apart as two of the largest generations in U.S. history—77 million Boomers and 82 million Millennials (National Conference on Citizenship n.d.). Civic engagement levels usually increase as individuals reach retirement age, when individuals have higher levels of community ties, greater resources, and larger networks. While this is the current phase of life for Boomers, Millennials are already a civic-minded generation that is different from Generation Xers. This can be witnessed and explained by increased voter participation by young adults in the 2008 elections.

When compared to Baby Boomers, young adult Millennials are slightly more likely to volunteer. But involvement and engagement look a little different for Millennials. Millennials are not likely to engage in face-to-face social engagement (National Conference on Citizenship n.d.). With the rise of the Internet, it is easier for individuals to be engaged and informed all from the comfort of their home. Online fund-raising and Facebook pages dedicated to raising awareness for a particular cause are more likely sources of involvement for younger generations. This should not be taken as apathy as Millennials are considered more engaged in nontraditional ways.

Organizations can provide opportunities for employees to engage in the community. Offering community service days or adopting particular causes can be positive ways to keep employees involved and allow them to connect personal satisfaction to the work environment. Giving employees time for volunteering or matching employee donations dollar for dollar are ways for organizations to provide employees with additional benefits. Employees may not see a direct dollar amount paid for their day of volunteering, but they won't suffer lost wages while giving their time.

Rates in social engagement do not differ by race and ethnicity for Millennials (see figure 3.1A/B/C). Volunteer rates for white and nonwhite Millennials is 56 percent, and voting rates are virtually the same as (National Conference on Citizenship n.d.). However, older generations have larger differences in volunteering and social engagement by race and ethnicity. Some of the enhanced rates among younger generations may be a result of larger involvement at both the high school and university levels. Students may have curriculum requirements that require community service. Even if this is the reason

Figure 3.1 **Ethnic Diversity in the United States**

A. Millenials, ages 18–29

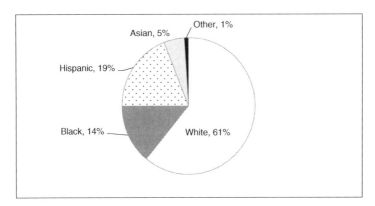

B. Adults, ages 30 and older

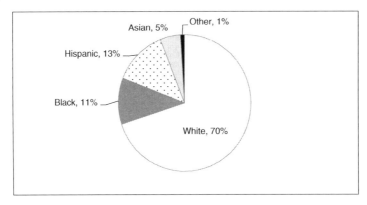

C. Race/Ethnicity, 2009 (% by generation)

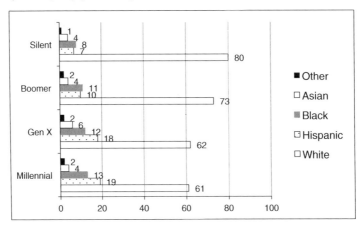

Note: All groups (other than Hispanic) are non-Hispanic.
Source: Paul Taylor and Scott Keeter (eds.), *Millennials: A Portrait of Generation Next* (Washington, DC: Pew Research Center, February 2010), www.pewsocialtrends.org/files/2010/10/millennials-confident-connected-open-to-change.pdf.

for increased involvement levels, it is a good predictor for the future. Civic engagement rates are closely related to the number of opportunities individuals have throughout their lives (National Conference on Citizenship n.d.).

Millennials are demonstrating higher rates of volunteerism. This may be a result of more exposure through school-based programs. Service learning and community service are both considered valuable to overall student development. In 1999, the U.S. Department of Education found that 46 percent of public high schools and 38 percent of middle schools offered service learning, while 83 percent of high schools and 77 percent of middle schools organized community service opportunities (Reingold and Nesbit 2006). In 1984, when Generation X would have been in high school and middle school, 9 percent of schools had service learning opportunities and 27 percent of public high schools had community service. The increased educational focus and inclusion of community service and service learning is helping to shape a generation of service-focused individuals. This carries over into the collegiate level. Volunteer rates are also related to college education. As the number of individuals receiving college degrees increases, volunteer rates increase as well. It is possible that because younger generations are staying in school longer and receiving more degrees, their exposure to and understanding of community service is higher overall (Wilson 2000). Millennials prefer volunteering for short-term commitments similar to their approach to the workplace (Achieve and Johnson, Grossnickle and Associates 2013). The chances for engagement span from one-time volunteering to long-term volunteer leadership roles.

Volunteer rates are increasing and have been on an upward trend since the Baby Boomer generation came of age. Increased college education and the fact that individuals are living longer are a couple of the reasons these rates have gone up. Some studies have even linked volunteer rates with better health outcomes and longevity in adults, so there may be a reciprocal relationship between the two (Reingold and Nesbit 2006). Baby Boomers and older Generation X members are also more likely to have school-aged children, which could increase the likelihood of involvement. Involving children in volunteer activities will increase the likelihood that volunteer rates hold steady, or perhaps increase. Organizations that are interested in having a supply of volunteers should provide opportunities for both older and younger volunteers simultaneously. Having programs where individuals of all ages can not only interact but also experience community service at the same time can help in all areas of life.

Diversity among the Millennial generation has increased in both the physical sense and in a much more technical way. Millennials are more likely to express themselves differently than generations before them. Instead of face-to-face interactions, they will look to social media and networking websites to post videos and written commentary (Taylor and Keeter 2010). Millennials are also more likely to have tattoos and piercings which speaks to their need and feelings for self-expression (Taylor and Keeter 2010). Millennials are half as likely to be married when compared to their parent's generation at the same age (Taylor and Keeter 2010). Similar to the Baby Boomer generation, Millennials are competitive in nature and feel pressure to keep up with their peers. Based on generational profiles millennials are also extremely brand loyal, and nonprofits can learn from the private sector in marketing directly to the needs and loyalties of younger generations. Much like their assumptions in the workplace, if younger generations aren't happy with their nonprofit organizations, they will move on or even create their own. This generation is solution-oriented and will find a place in which to fit.

Today, nonprofit organizations need to evaluate the way they engage potential donors. If direct mailings and phone calls are historically the main ways organizations contact donors and volunteers, then different forms might be necessary to maintain older generations, while engaging a new generation of supporters. Preferred forms of communications are increasingly moving to online forms, websites, e-mails and e-newsletters. Millennials are more likely to engage in promoting their charities to others by forwarding e-mails or posting on social networks.

Fund-raising overall has changed in how it is conducted. Preston (2010) found that 30 percent of people would support fund-raising efforts via text. Many nonprofits rely on financial contributions and volunteers, but Millennials are less likely to give as much or as often as other generations (See Figure 3.2). It could be the result of a lack of financial

Figure 3.2   **Average Charitable Contributions by Generational Groups per Year**

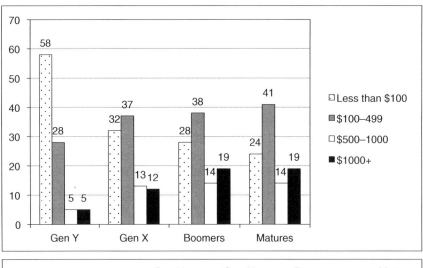

	Gen Y	Gen X	Boomers	Matures
Avg $ (est.)	$341	$796	$901	$1066
Avg $ top charity	$161	$272	$211	$280
Average # charities	3.6	4.2	5.2	6.3

Source: Vinay Bhagat, Pam Loeb, and Mark Rovner, *The Next Generation of American Giving: A Study on the Contrasting Charitable Habits of Generation Y, Generation X, Baby Boomers and Matures* (Arlington, VA: Edge Research, 2010), www.edgeresearch.com/Edge%20Research%20Case%20 Study%20-%20Next-Gen-Whitepaper.pdf (accessed on January 21, 2014).

stability and/or not feeling comfortable giving financially. Younger generations may find giving time or spreading information are more cost effective ways to participate. So, if giving monetarily is a function of life cycle, this may increase as they get older. Millennials are more likely to give online versus in person or by mail (Achieve and Johnson, Grossnickle and Associates 2013).

Millennials overall are an optimistic generation and, to the extent possible (See Figure 3.3), want to make the world a better place (Center on Philanthropy at Indiana University 2008). This is a great resource for nonprofits to take advantage of. If organizations would start contacts early and often in cheaper, more direct outlets, it is likely they would be able to find long-term resources. Millennials will be attracted to secular organizations, but this does not mean religious organizations are out of the play for this group. This young group wants to better the world, and they want to help others. Financial contributions may be lower, but when giving money, this generation is more comfortable with online giving.

Another resource nonprofits can take advantage of with younger generations is the likelihood that they are well educated. When these individuals give back, they may be a greater organizational resource. Some of the advanced skills that younger workers have

Figure 3.3   **Top Ten Phrases to Describe Millennials**

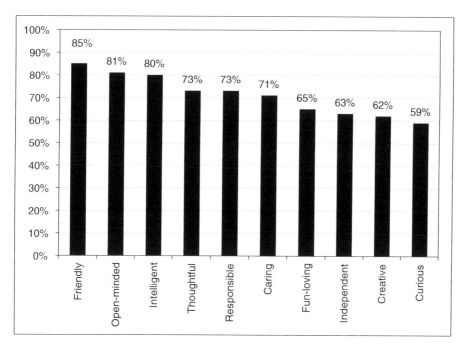

Source: Cone Inc., and AMP Agency, *The 2006 Cone Millennial Cause Study—The Millennial Generation: Pro-Social and Empowered to Change the World* (Boston: Cone Communications, 2006), www.greenbook.org/Content/AMP/Cause_AMPlified.pdf (accessed on January 22, 2014).

can help supplement full-time staff. This may not be in the form of internships but in the form of assignments and contracting out certain projects. Individuals may be looking for ways to build portfolios, so doing volunteer graphic design work or program assessment could be a new way to involve younger workers in volunteer work. Traditional programs work for some individuals, but the younger generation may want to give and still remain at arm's length from actual interaction. Giving volunteers social media responsibility is one example of how one can give time, but that time may not be directly in contact with the organization. Just as jobs allow individuals to telecommute, nonprofits and foundations can have the same system for volunteers.

To appeal to Millennials, nonprofit organizations should have clear and concise websites. These websites should include a call to action and photos that should say exactly what type of services they provide (Achieve and Johnson, Grossnickle and Associates 2013). Using websites can also be a way to post opportunities for involvement. Organizations can post volunteer opportunities along with board memberships especially suited for younger members. Organizations interested in finding out the needs and interests of younger individuals can also engage them in board positions. If large financial investments are a general barrier for involvement of younger members, they should be waived if the younger members possess certain skills that are needed for the organizations. Organizations can implement young professional nonprofit boards that could translate into traditional board policy. Some Millennials will not want to make the long-term commitment required by board positions, so it might be a good way to highlight future leadership potential.

Although nonprofits should seek the skills of younger volunteers, they should not ignore the skills of Baby Boomers. Baby Boomers will also be seeking challenging opportunities, and they may have more time for volunteering after they have retired. Taking full advantage of their skills is a great way to get valuable service from their experiences. The availability of volunteering opportunities is also related to the financial giving of Boomers. Organizations wishing to establish clear channels of giving can also increase volunteer opportunities.

VOLUNTEERING FOR THE AGES: YOUNG PROFESSIONALS, TEENAGERS, AND SENIOR PROGRAMS

Age-specific volunteering takes into account the different life stages of individuals (see Figure 3.4). Millennials, Generations X/Y, and Baby Boomers will all want different activities at certain stages of life. Many organizations are trying to appeal to Generation Y and Millennials. A trend of making volunteering and giving back more hip and fun can be achieved with young professional and youth networks. These networks usually target people under the age of 40 and have different types of volunteer activities. The traditional Saturday morning or after-work mentoring takes a different form in this case. Young professional networks might have happy hours or other nontraditional means of interaction. Individuals may be able to raise money for an organization by running in a marathon or participating in other activities. Organizations benefit because they have people raising awareness for their cause. The individuals benefit because they get to

Figure 3.4 **Adult Volunteering (in %)**

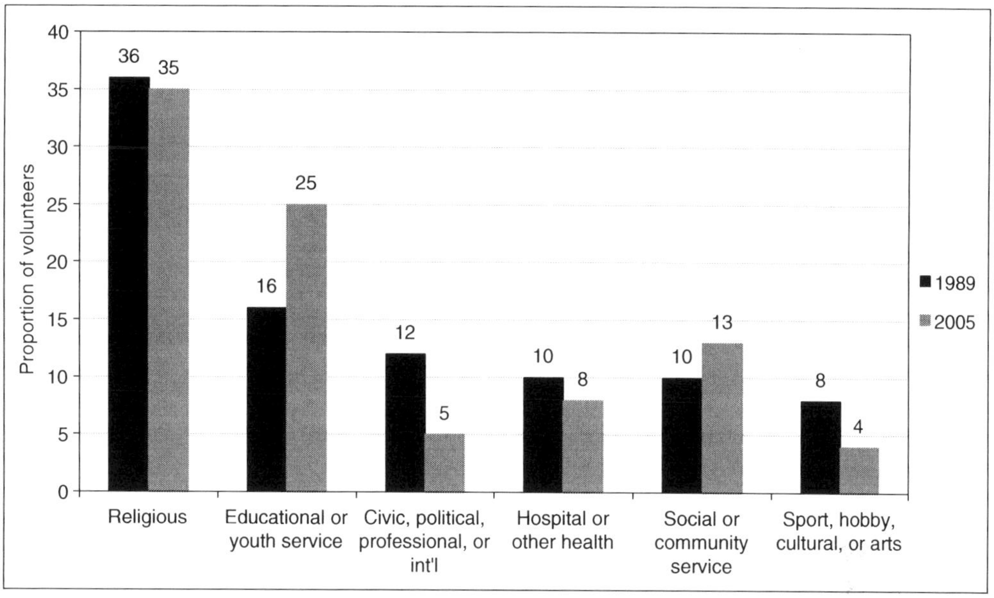

Sources: David Reingold and Rebecca Nesbit, *Volunteer Growth in America: A Review of Trends Since 1974* (Washington, DC: Corporation for National and Community Service, December 2006), www. nationalservice.gov/pdf/06_1203_volunteer_growth.pdf (accessed on January 22, 2014); John Wilson, "Volunteering," *Annual Review Sociology* 26 (2000): 215–240.

give back while working within the confines of their current comfort area. Many of these young professional networks rely on social media to spread the word about their programs.

Young professional volunteer organizations provide individuals with an opportunity to network with others with similar interests. Individuals can expand their networks both professionally and socially. It might be easier for a young professional to gather a few friends and attend an after-work happy hour where the proceeds benefit a nonprofit organization than to get friends to do a service project on a Saturday morning. Bringing the opportunity to give back directly to the people will be a major benefit for organizations. While a happy hour may not seem like a traditional means of volunteering, it provides a great opportunity for fund-raising as well as a way to increase the organization's exposure.

Many organizations such as the American Red Cross, Big Brothers Big Sisters, and Habitat for Humanity have young professional networks. These organizations try to combine service with networking and other social events to attract young volunteers and donors. It may be some time before they actually sign on the individuals as monthly volunteers, but the organization's name will be on those individuals' radar. The hope would be when they are ready to give time, talents, and resources to an organization, it will be that which they were exposed to as a young professional.

DoSomething.org

DoSomething.org is a program that targets young people and tries to increase their level and interest in volunteering. This excerpt from their website gives a clue about the message they are sending:

> DoSomething.org is the country's largest not-for-profit for young people and social change. We have 2.5 million members (and counting!) who kick ass on causes they care about. Bullying. Animal cruelty. Homelessness. Cancer. The list goes on. DoSomething.org spearheads national campaigns so 13- to 25-year-olds can make an impact-without ever needing money, an adult, or a car. Over 2.4 million people took action through DoSomething.org in 2012. Why? Because apathy sucks.
>
> (DoSomething.org n.d.a)

This organization is using language, tone, and enthusiasm to attract young people. They value young people acting and engaging without waiting for established organizations. The idea for DoSomething.org is that formal organizations place a barrier on involvement. Many of the programs are directed at issues uniquely tailored to the age group (bullying, hunger, and money management). This is an organization that respects and values the talents of young people and sees them as leaders first.

The top 11 reasons for volunteering for this age group (DoSomething.org n.d.b):

1. Having friends who volunteer regularly is the primary factor influencing a teen's volunteering habits.
2. 40 percent of young people who volunteered in 2011 did so with clubs, friends, family, or on their own. They did not go through a traditional "organization."
3. Teens want volunteering to feel like a party; the activities should be social.
4. More than 70 percent of young people with friends who regularly volunteer also volunteer.
5. The number one concern for students is paying for college. After that, their concern is getting accepted.
6. Young people want to volunteer with people their age, but not the same gender.
7. Lack of time is the number one reason teens give for not volunteering.
8. Many young people want to remain anonymous or help from a distance.
9. For religious youth, volunteering habits aren't determined by the importance of religion in their life. Rather, such habits are determined by how frequently they attend religious events, including youth groups.
10. Young people want volunteer opportunities that are close to home, but not at home.
11. Short-term activities that allow for different levels of engagement are best (five minutes versus an hour versus half a day).

From the list, there is an emphasis on volunteering collectively and as an individual. Individuals want to feel connected and a part of something with their friends, even if it is just for a few minutes. This prepares individuals for the next level of young professional engagement.

Covenant House Florida–The Young Professionals

Here is an example of a recent ad from the Covenant House of Florida website:

> The Young Professionals for Covenant House is a group of business professionals who attend monthly social, networking, and sporting events and activities to raise money and awareness for Covenant House Florida.
>
> Mingle at the best bars and restaurants, join our volleyball league, cruise to some of the most beautiful and fun destinations, and attend annual events such as . . . Cranberry Jam, Covenant House Florida 5K on A1A, Mardi Gras Bash, Fort Lauderdale Bus Loop, Hard Rock Pub Crawls, and more!

Some of the activities that the YP plan across the country include "Sleep Outs," where supporters spend one night sleeping outside to raise the awareness of homeless youth; fund-raising happy hours; and 5K, half, and full marathons where individuals can run on behalf of the Covenant House team. These activities are targeted toward younger individuals who are social, active, and engaged (See Figure 3.5). The benefit is that volunteers get to do activities they might not do otherwise and attach their efforts to a good cause.

Figure 3.5 **Connect. Involve. Give.**

Connect

- Make sure your website and online communications are mobile-friendly, but also make sure they offer real information and illustrate clearly the organization's impact.
- Don't put your technology eggs all in one basket. Cultivate multiple communication channels.
- Embrace social media. But not at the expense of clear, concise and meaningful information.
- Maintain a smartphone-friendly website that delivers clear information about your organization and how to get involved.

Involve

- Facilitate quick access to information and make it easy for people to share details with others.
- Let people know how donations are used, and share with them real stories of the organization's impact.
- Cultivate networks of champions and make it easy for engaged people to share information and engage others.
- Offer Millennials real opportunities to join in leadership, and provide a range of volunteer experiences.

Give

- Create a website and social media presence that makes it easy for donors to give as inspiration strikes.
- Deliver tangible transparency, describing in literal terms what donors' gifts will do for the organization—what the money will buy or support.
- Equip your Millennial donors to solicit donors from others.
- Ask . . . for donations, for volunteers and for Millennials to serve as your champions.

Source: Achieve and Johnson, Grossnickle and Associates, *The Millennial Impact Report 2012* (Indianapolis: Achieve, 2013), 34, http://cdn.trustedpartner.com/docs/library/Achieve MCON2013/TheMillennialImpactReport2012.pdf (accessed on January 22, 2014).

Senior Corps

Senior Corps is a division of the AmeriCorps program. It is an organization for individuals age 55 and older who wish to be active and give back to their communities. Programs like Foster Grandparents and Senior Companions help seniors give their time and talents to programs tailored especially for them. As discussed previously, this age group possesses a wealth of knowledge, skill, and information, and they should be able to serve. Young professional or evening programs will not always appeal to this group. However, programs that allow daytime activities or programs close to their home can be appealing to this group. Connecting individuals with community, nonprofit, faith-based, and other service groups is the main focus of the Senior Corps program.

POINTS TO REMEMBER

- Attract younger generations by providing group volunteer opportunities; combine social opportunities for individuals to get involved.
- Balance the need for finances and monetary contributions; organizations need money, but they should not present challenges for anyone interested in serving from being involved.
- Allow volunteers to have more responsibility; don't be afraid to delegate to promising volunteers. Increased responsibility and involvement is great way to keep individuals coming back.
- Use social media platforms for connections; the outlets are endless to send and receive volunteer opportunities with interested volunteers.
- Provide one-time and long-term commitment; individuals may want to give any amount of time to volunteering—from minutes to days. Organizations will benefit from allowing diverse time commitments for potential volunteers.
- Provide spots on boards for young members (remove financial barriers). This may attract individuals earlier on in their careers and hopefully encourage lifelong participation and giving to organizations.
- Provide multiple options for individuals to give: financial, time, social media, blogging, and other talents; the list is endless. Let people give in the manner that best suits them.

4

Communicating with Generation Next

Communication and feedback are important in any work environment. Managers and employees need to know that different groups may have different expectations on how proper feedback is defined. Older employees may believe that one management style is best, but the hope is that the best is being pulled out of employees, and managers should support employees in doing so. Generational differences mean that individuals of different ages have different values, ideas, ways of getting things done, and communicating presents an interesting new challenge. Differences based on race, gender, age, ethnicity, and religion have long existed. So dealing with generations shouldn't be a problem. But generational differences present a unique diversity challenge. Roles in the current workplace have shifted, and the rules are being rewritten (Hammill 2005).

People often communicate based on the backgrounds associated with their generations (Hammill 2005). Many of the habits, motivational cues, expectations, and behaviors developed by humans have something to do with the time and background in which they grew up. Understanding how to communicate with different generations may lessen workplace conflicts, confrontations, and employee turnover (Hammill 2005). Generational differences can be seen in school, at work, and in the home (please see Table 4.1). Managing the conflicts or learning ways to prevent conflicts all together is important for managers and employees.

PERSONAL AND LIFESTYLE CHARACTERISTICS BY GENERATION

Some of the differences in communication can be influenced by advances in technology. Some of the generational similarities and differences in the workplace can be seen in Tables 4.2 and 4.3. Traditionalists are more inclined to use written one-on-one communication, and Generation Yers are more inclined to use e-mail and Internet communication (Hammill 2005). In the middle, Baby Boomers are considered more accessible at the workplace, while Generation Yers feel that work should be left at work. Communication and work-life balance play a strong role in socializing and motivation at the workplace. While one group may want to set up meetings in person, another group may

Table 4.1

10+ Ways to Minimize Generational Differences in the Workplace

Action No.	Description of Action
1	Focus on similarities rather than differences
2	Recognize that change does occur
3	Recognize the value and the perils of the "tried and true"
4	Be aware that "new" technology may not be
5	Develop a curiosity for things unknown to you
6	Ask questions rather than make statements
7	Avoid characterizations based on age
8	Define your acronyms
9	Paraphrase before answering
10	Be careful about cultural or historical references
11	If that other age-group worker was right after all, say so

Source: Calvin Sun, "10+ Ways to Minimize Generational Differences in the Workplace," *Tech Republic*, January 18, 2011, www.techrepublic.com/blog/10-things/10-plus-ways-to-minimize-generational-differences-in-the-workplace/ (accessed November 22, 2013).

see this as unnecessary and inconvenient for younger generations, who are less likely to want the person-to-person contact. In the workplace, it may be more efficient for managers to use a variety of communication styles that are effective for the different types of employees. Video and telephone conferencing may be preferable to some employees, and advances in technology should be used in the workplace.

TRAINING AND LEARNING STYLES

Learning methods can be separated into soft and hard skills. Soft skills are those attributes that make a person unique. Hard skills can often be learned or trained for. Soft skills give people a slight edge if they are requirements of a position (for example, communication skills or social graces). Training can be an important factor in employee retention and commitment, and it should be used as a tool for managers. Traditionalists and Baby Boomers are more likely to prefer on-the-job training for soft skills, and hard skills should be taught in classroom settings. Younger generations thrive on feedback and want it often. Direct job-specific training is favored by older generations, while younger generations prefer general leadership training that could be taken to any future employment opportunities (Deal 2007). Younger generations will not need as much

Table 4.2

Generational Differences in Work-Related Characteristic and Expectations

	Traditionals	Baby Boomers	Generation X	Generation Y
Work ethic	Hard-working	Workaholic	Only work as hard as needed	
Attitudes toward authority/rules	• They value conformity, authority and rules, and a top-down management approach • 13% included authority among their top 10 values	• Some may still be uncomfortable interacting with authority figures[1] • 5% included authority among their top 10 values[2]	• They are comfortable with authorities and are not impressed with titles or intimidated by them[3] • They find it natural to interact with their superiors • 6% included authority in their top 10 values	• They believe that respect must be earned[4] • 6% included authority in their top 10 values[1]
Expectations regarding respect[1]	• Deference • Special treatment • More weight given to their opinions	• Deference • Special treatment • More weight given to their opinions	• They want to be held in esteem • They want to be listened to • They do not expect deference	• They want to be held in esteem • They want to be listened to • They do not expect deference
Preferred way to learn soft skills[1]	• On the job • Discussion groups • Peer interaction and feedback • Classroom instruction, live • One-on-one job coaching	• On the job • Discussion groups • One-on-one coaching • Classroom instruction, live • Peer interaction and feedback	• On the job • One-on-one coaching • Peer interaction and feedback • Assessment and feedback • Discussion groups	• On the job • Peer interaction and feedback • Discussion groups • One-on-one coaching • Assessment and feedback
Preferred way to learn hard skills	• Classroom instruction, live • On the job • Workbooks and manuals • Books and reading • One-on-one coaching/ computer-based training	• Classroom instruction, live • On the job • Workbooks and manuals • Books and reading • One-on-one coaching	• On the job • Classroom instruction, live • Workbooks and manuals • Books and reading • One-on-one coaching	• On the job • Classroom instruction, live • Workbooks and manuals • Books and reading • One-on-one coaching

(Continued)

Table 4.2

(Continued)

	Traditionals	Baby Boomers	Generation X	Generation Y
Feedback and supervision	Attitudes closer to Boomers	May be insulted by continuous feedback	Immediate and continuous	Immediate and continuous
Attitudes regarding loyalty to their employer	• Considered among the most loyal workers[1] • About 70% of those interviewed would like to stay with their organization for the rest of their working life[5]	• They value company commitment and loyalty[1] • About 65% of those interviewed would like to stay with their organization for the rest of their working life[6]	• Less loyal to companies than previous generations but loyal to people[1] • About 40% of those interviewed would like to stay with their organization for the rest of their working life[7]	• Committed and loyal when dedicated to an idea, cause, or product[8] • About 20% of those interviewed would like to stay with their organization for the rest of their working life[1]
Work/life balance		Sacrificed personal life for work	Valued work-life balance	Value work-life balance?
Perceived elements of success in the workplace[4]	• Meet deadlines (80%) • Willingness to learn new things (84%) • Get along with people (81%) • Use computer (78%) • Speak clearly and concisely (78%)	• Use computer (82%) • Willingness to learn new things (80%) • Get along with people (78%) • Meet deadlines (77%) • Organizational skills (73%)	• Use computer (79%) • Meet deadlines (75%) • Willingness to learn new things (74%) • Speak clearly and concisely (72%) • Get along with people (71%)	• Use computer (66%) • Meet deadlines (62%) • Multitasking (59%) • Willingness to learn new things (58%) • Speak clearly and concisely (55%)
Top developmental areas[1]	• Skills training in my areas of expertise • Computer training • Team building	• Skills training in my areas of expertise • Leadership • Computer training	• Leadership • Skills training in my areas of expertise • Team building	• Leadership • Problem solving, decision making • Skills training in my areas of expertise
Preferred leadership attributes[9]	• Credible (65%) • Listens well (59%) • Trusted (59%)	• Credible (74%) • Trusted (61%) • Farsighted (57%)	• Credible (71%) • Trusted (58%) • Farsighted (54%)	• Listens well (68%) • Dependable (66%) • Dedicated (63%)

Source: Anick Tolbize, *Generation Differences in the Workplace* (Minneapolis: University of Minnesota, August 16, 2008), 11–12.

[1] Deal 2007.
[2] Karp, Fuller, and Siras 2002: National Oceanographic and Atmospheric Association Office of Diversity 2006.
[3] Karp et al. 2002: Valueoptons.com; Zemke, Raines and Filipczak 2000; Jenkins 2007.
[4] Valueoptions.com.
[5] Jenkins 2007; Valueoptions.com; Zemke et al. 2002.
[6] Jorgensen 2003; Karp et al. 2002; Yu and Miller 2005.
[7] Crampton and Hodge 2006; Jorgensen 2003; National Oceanographic and Atmospheric Association Office of Diversity 2006; Kopfer 2004.
[8] Karp et al. 2002; Jorgensen 2003.
[9] Randstad Work Solutions 2007.

Table 4.3

Elements on Which Members of Each Generation Are Mostly Similar

	Traditionals	Baby Boomers	Generation X	Generation Y
Concerns related to change[1]	• Doing the same work with fewer resources • Changes in both the internal and external environment • Technology changes • Change that is disorganized, unnecessary, or both • Resistance to change	Similar	Similar	Similar
Reasons for staying in an organization[1]	• Opportunity to advance within the organization • Learning and development • Respect and recognition • Better quality of life • Better compensation	Similar	Similar	Similar
Attitudes toward teamwork	Likes teamwork	Likes teamwork	Likes teamwork	Likes teamwork
Attitudes regarding flexibility[2]	• Freedom to set own hours if the work gets done (76%) • Working full-time for a firm (64%) • Full-time job with extended time off as needed for personal reasons (46%) • Four-day workweek with 10-hour days (44%)	• Freedom to set own hours if the work gets done (74%) • Working full-time for a firm (64%) • Four-day workweek with 10-hour days (58%) • Full-time job with extended time off as needed for personal reasons (56%)	• Freedom to set own hours if the work gets done (73%) • Working full-time for a firm (63%) • Full-time job with extended time off as needed for personal reasons (59%) • Four-day workweek with 10-hour days (52%)	• Freedom to set own hours if the work gets done (63%) • Full-time job with extended time off as needed for personal reasons (53%) • Working full-time for a firm (50%) • Four-day workweek with 10-hour days (32%)

(Continued)

Table 4.3

(Continued)

	Traditionals	Baby Boomers	Generation X	Generation Y
Most important aspects of workplace culture[2]	• Fair (90%) • Ethical (90%) • Straightforward (74%) • Professional (74%) • Collaborative/team feeling (65%)	• Fair (86%) • Ethical (84%) • Straightforward (76%) • Professional (70%) • Collaborative/team feeling (70%)	• Fair (87%) • Ethical (83%) • Straightforward (74%) • Collaborative/team feeling (65%) • Friendly/social (65%)	• Fair (66%) • Ethical (66%) • Friendly/social (59%) • Straightforward (54%) • Professional (48%)
Communication tools used for work[2]	• Desktop computer (87%) • Landline phone (87%) • Fax (78%) • Mobile/cell phone (73%) • Laptop computer (43%) • PDAs with phone and Internet (11%)	• Desktop computer (81%) • Landline phone (84%) • Fax (74%) • Mobile/cell phone (66%) • Laptop computer (44%) • PDAs with phone and Internet (15%)	• Desktop computer (75%) • Landline phone (81%) • Fax (65%) • Mobile/cell phone (65%) • Laptop computer (44%) • PDAs with phone and Internet (15%)	• Desktop computer (71%) • Landline phone (67%) • Fax (52%) • Mobile/cell phone (46%) • Laptop computer (26%) • PDAs with phone and Internet (6%)
Top values[3]	• Family (46%) • Integrity (46%) • Love (26%)	• Family (45%) • Integrity (32%) • Love (27%)	• Family (67%) • Love (32%) • Integrity (24%)	• Family (73%) • Love (49%) • Spirituality (28%)
Top reasons for happiness in the work place[2]	• Feeling valued (88%) • Recognition and appreciation (84%) • Supportive environment (70%) • Leadership I can relate to (69%) • Shared vision, values and pride (63%)	• Feeling valued (87%) • Recognition and appreciation (78%) • Supportive environment (71%) • Leadership I can relate to (71%) • Capable workforce (64%)	• Feeling valued (84%) • Recognition and appreciation (74%) • Supportive environment (69%) • Capable workforce (68%) • Leadership I can relate to (66%)	• Feeling valued (85%) • Recognition and appreciation (74%) • Supportive environment (73%) • Capable workforce (72%) • Being part of a team (68%)

Source: Anick Tolbize, *Generation Differences in the Workplace* (Minneapolis: University of Minnesota, August 16, 2008), 11–12.

[1] Deal 2007.

[2] Randstad 2007.

[3] Deal 2007, Kersten 2002; Valueoptions.com; National Oceanographic and Atmospheric Association Office of Diversity 2006; Zemke, Raines, and Filipczak 2000.

technology training because they adapt quickly and are used to new technology being introduced in their lifetime. Traditionalists may need training for new and existing technology. Much like benefits packages that are not one-size-fits-all, training should be seen as an à la carte organizational need. Managers should take advantage of the skills their own employees provide. Matching younger and older generations could be beneficial and cost effective for organizations. Younger generations can contribute their technology expertise, and older generations can pass along their experience and leadership knowledge. Setting up peer-to-peer mentor groups or job rotations can help pass along skills without formal training programs or distractions from day-to-day work schedules. Training does not have to be a formal classroom activity, but employee needs should be assessed. If these needs are met, they can help employees feel connected and valued in the organization.

ATTITUDES TOWARD COMMUNICATION

Around-the-clock communications versus workplace-only contact is a common issue along the generational line. Older generations see work as a means to end while younger generations strive for a greater work-life balance. As discussed previously, the Baby Boom generation is one of the largest and most competitive of the four generations. Baby Boomers are present, engaged in work, and available at all times (Hammill 2005). Gen Xers and Traditionalists see work as a part of a larger life that includes family and friends and will not be as responsive or eager to seek work outside of office hours. Younger generations will, however, have longer hours of availability due to their higher levels of technological connectivity. Traditionalists, Baby Boomers, and Generation Y managers should know that being present may not always mean that workers are doing their best work. It may be better for younger workers to work nontraditional schedules.

Many sources of conflict can arise from the misunderstood *perceptions* of generations more so than *real* differences which can be seen in differences of expectations in Table 4.4. A successful intergenerational workplace will have many open and direct communications to handle conflicts face-to-face. Respect is viewed differently across generations, so employees and employers should be aware of this. An organization's culture should promote open and direct dialogue in the workplace.

Communication styles vary greatly across generations. There are more avenues of communication available, but it can become increasingly difficult due to the influence of technology on communication (Elmore 2012). In the workplace, a lack of proper communication can cause information to be spread inaccurately. This can be a detriment to the organization's efficiency. Face-to-face communication can be a lost art for a generation that is used to electronic communication. Because of the existence of social media and a heavy reliance on text messaging, communication in the workplace isn't limited to what may have existed 20 years ago. This transfers to the workplace where some prefer face-to-face interaction and others prefer electronic communication.

Table 4.4

Employers and Employees

Parents, educators, mentors and employers are being challenged by the new rules and a language we literally don't understand. We are immigrants in this new world of young natives. Even though we desire to connect, communicating with the next generation provides unique challenges. For instance contrast corporate America with her newest employee, a fresh college graduate:

Most Employers Tend to . . .	Most Young Employees Tend to . . .
1. Email information to colleagues	1. Facebook information to colleagues
2. Use a phone to call people	2. Use a phone to text people
3. Relay data thru a one-way download	3. Learn best thru uploading/interacting
4. Prefer copy and words to report facts	4. Love images to report/receive facts
5. Leap into "what" others must know	5. Want to grasp "why" they must know
6. View the world via facts and figures	6. View the world via stories and feelings

Source: Tim Elmore, "In Other Words: Learning the Art of Communicating with the Next Generation," *Growing Leaders*, January 6, 2012, http://growingleaders.com/blog/in-other-words/ (accessed January 20, 2014).

Understanding the communication gap is critical. As a result of our reliance on technology for communication, there has been a breakdown in understanding nonverbal cues (see differences and advice in Table 4.5 and 4.6). The lack of focused attention during meetings and classes shows how employees are only engaged in whatever is going on in the moment. Technology encourages "continuous partial attention" because often people are texting, responding to e-mail, and surfing the Internet during times when they are around others doing the same (Bauerlein 2009). Younger generations may see no problem with sending a quick text message during a meeting, but they do not understand that they are perceived through nonverbal cues to be distracted and disinterested. Organizations should consider having meetings where nonessential forms of technology are banned. This presents an environment that forces engagement and awareness. This is one place where perception can mean everything. Even if an individual is on the phone or surfing the web during a meeting, he may just be looking up something that is relevant to the discussion. Since we do not know the nature of the person's phone usage, we often assume that he is texting or doing something not related to the discussion. This is why a general "no tech" rule is good for all in the beginning. Initially, there may be some blowback because we are so reliant on phones and laptops. (This is also discussed in the discussion in chapter 7 regarding classroom engagement.)

The youngest generation in the workforce is used to—and in need of—constant communication. They are the product of a generation that was raised while technology was exploding and reaching new heights. This may pose a problem for some managers. When asked about generational differences, a veteran New Jersey State Trooper said that

Table 4.5

Students and Schools

The same gap often exists between students today and the typical classroom. Communicating with the next generation is a challenge for teachers as kids have been conditioned to be participatory, but most faculty don't teach that way:

Students Today	Schools Today
1. Right-brain thinkers	1. Left-brain delivery
2. Experiential in nature	2. Passive in nature
3. Learn by uploading, expressing themselves	3. Teach by downloading lectures
4. Music / art enable them to retain information	4. Music and art classes often cut
5. Desire to learn what is relevant to life	5. Teach for the next test
6. Creativity drives them	6. Curricula/test scores drive them

Source: Tim Elmore, "In Other Words: Learning the Art of Communicating with the Next Generation," *Growing Leaders*, January 6, 2012, http://growingleaders.com/blog/in-other-words/ (accessed January 20, 2014).

Table 4.6

Communicating with Digital Natives

7	Understand the audience
6	Listen to the conversation
5	Challenge the norms
4	Embrace technology
3	Be interesting and unique
2	Create real opportunities to participate
1	Think ten years ahead

Source: Nick Skytland, "7 Tips to Effectively Communicate with the Next Generation," *open.NASA*, December 4, 2011, http://open.nasa.gov/blog/2011/12/04/7-tips-to-effectively-communicate-with-the-next-generation/ (accessed January 20, 2014).

younger troopers call for directions versus using their discretion. These young troopers call to get clearance before making decisions. This could be part of the Millennials' need for confirmation and approval, but technology has also allowed rapid response, which this generation values. Dashboard cameras and audio recordings make new troopers suspicious of mistakes, and technology allows them the convenience of getting approval. There is an expectation of communication anywhere, anytime, and anyplace. This may make older veteran troopers annoyed or inconvenienced, but they need to understand that it is a generational trend to need immediate feedback and approval, and technology in communication has allowed it. Managers noticing such trends should find ways to ensure that individuals do not rely on technology crutches in their jobs when they should instead exercise their own discretion.

Millennials have an expectation of quick response, which is a function of their lives being filled with convenience and flexibility. Communication and time commitments are flexible and endless. Millennials also have an expectation that organizations will provide them with the same kind of flexibility. In the workplace, communication and technology help younger workers because they are likely to use their time efficiently and are experienced at multitasking. However, they also expect instant gratification, so delays or responses that are not instantaneous will be challenging to them (see complete list of differences in Table 4.7).

The next generations will always be digital natives. Digital natives are those born knowing technology as a means of communication. In the workplace, everyone must find common ground. Giving organizations a communication assessment is not just something for the organization internally, but can also be done to assess how the organization communicates with those outside of the organization. External communication can be with stakeholders, clients, citizens, donors, and service providers. Technology can help bring others into the organization. Websites and social media may need to be updated and enhanced to reflect changes in the external environment and changes in technology. The time of government organizations simply giving information has passed. Future generations will want interactive communication and new forms of contact even with organizations that usually refrain from making comments. Even if this nonverbal communicating with the next generation is an art and skill, it will be a valuable tool to learn. Organizations should engage all generations when developing communication strategies (see Table 4.8 on ways to foster communication and mutual understanding). This may take more time, but it might not be financially expensive, and the return on investment could be endless.

Traditionalists are far more likely than younger generations to want personal interaction and formal communication. This is a place where young and old might collide. Younger generations are the texting generation, and it is necessary for them to know that slang and text type is not acceptable when communicating in the workplace. However, if communications in the corporate culture are more relaxed, then older generations will have to know that this is a common practice and not that younger worker are not taking work seriously. Traditionalists want a work environment that involves respect, definite roles, and clear direction (Lechman n.d.). Baby Boomers need communication to affirm their position and show them recognition. They are used to communication and working in teams as a means to achieve more and to help with advancement. Generation Xers need hands-off communication and flexibility. They will complete tasks and often along the way ask for opinions, insight, and feedback. Managers of Gen Xers must be ready to provide feedback when it is wanted and this will frequently be given in a more informal

Table 4.7

Communicating Across Generations

Silent Generation Values

- Hard work
- Organization
- Hierarchy
- Tradition
- Logic
- Family
- Responsibility
- Honor
- Respect/obedience for authority
- Consistency, uniformity
- Discipline
- Financial and social conservatism

Managing Silents

- Acknowledge their experience
- Title is important
- Do not act intimidated
  - Address difficult topics
  - Allow time for preparation
- Use personal interaction
- Formal communication

Generational Feedback

- Silents—no news is good news
- Boomers—feedback once per year and lots of documentation
- Xers—sorry to interrupt, but how am I doing?
- Nexters—Feedback whenever I want it at the push of a button.

Source: Kathy Lechman, "Communicating Across Generations," (Columbus, OH: The Ohio State University Extension, n.d.), http://extensionhr.osu.edu/profdev/Microsoft%20PowerPoint%20-%20 Communicating%20Across%20Generations%20Presentation% 20for%20Web%20Ex%20May%2013,%202010%20Power%20 Point.pdf (accessed January 20, 2014).

Table 4.8

Initiatives to foster mutual support and understanding between Millennials and their managers can be advanced through the implementation of *two types of training* (Levit and Licina 2011):

1. Provide training on intergenerational dynamics which offers concrete strategies to build a better sense of community within teams.

2. Provide "soft-skill training for Millennial hires" that addresses such issues as:

   a. Assimilating into a new workplace culture;

   b. Working with team members assertively and diplomatically;

   c. Learning how to receive and process feedback;

   d. Learning how to approach a supervisor to seek mentorship and set long-term career goals; and

   e. Developing strategies to combat misperceptions about Millennials, such as reverse mentoring to more effectively leverage their strengths.

Source: Levit and Licina 2011.

and regular manner. When communicating with Millennials, it is important to show them respect (to be explained later), to give them challenges, and to lead by example.

Feedback is a necessary process of any organization or person growing and changing. Each generation wants feedback in different ways, and organizations should know this when trying to recruit and retain workers. Traditionalists prefer little to no feedback and will assume that if they are not being corrected, then they are on the correct path. Boomers want formal feedback on a scheduled basis. They are the generation most likely to prefer annual reviews. Generation Xers and beyond seek out feedback. Managers should not see this as a need for approval, but as a need for course correction. The younger generations want feedback on demand. They are used to getting what they want anytime and anyplace, and they do not leave this need for urgency behind when they enter the workplace. Silence is often confused with disapproval for Millennials (Lechman n.d.), with communication and feedback going hand in hand.

Communication failures can present a large cost to organizations. Turnover, complaints, and perceptions of unfairness and bias can all be attributed to communication failures. These failures can disrupt organizational flow and prevent efficiency. Organizations that divide work among teams should pay attention to how and when feedback is given. Intergenerational teams could present challenges for managers because different individuals may seek feedback in a variety of ways. Feedback along the way and at times of completion may be necessary.

In the workplace, formal communications and titles are preferred by the Traditionalist generation. The need for formality in communication then decreases a little with each of the successive generations. Boomers are slightly more informal and can receive information in less traditional environments. Generation Xers want quick and direct communication. E-mail or voice mail is fine for this group, and it is often the most straightforward and efficient way to disseminate information for them. Millennials want communication to be an acknowledgement of achievements. It is important to note that both positive and negative feedback are important. While younger generations may crave and want positive feedback, it is important that negative feedback be given when necessary. Performance standards cannot vary based on generational lines. Organizations should maintain the highest levels of equity and fairness when dealing with people of any generation.

ITEMS TO CONSIDER WHEN COMMUNICATING

Employers should always make sure that individuals are on the same page when communicating, especially in connection with the use of acronyms and initialisms. Text message lingo has made its way into mainstream communication even in professional settings. "LOL" is a common response to many messages. When communicating across generations, it might be necessary to define the difference between "Lots Of Love" and "Laugh Out Loud." As mentioned in this chapter, conflicts happen when not everyone is working with the same assumptions and background. Defining the language that each party is using will be helpful in avoiding potential conflicts.

Another practice that can help reduce the number of intergenerational communication conflicts is paraphrasing before responding. Doing this confirms for both parties that they have been heard and understood correctly before the conversation proceeds. Introducing this practice into the workplace may add an additional step to conversations, but it can save time in the long run. Asking follow-up questions is something that individuals at all levels of the organization should incorporate into daily interaction, especially when communicating instantaneously over written communications (like instant messenger). Text and instant messages provide no tone of voice, and often we read our own assumptions into such messages. Some groups may be able to easily disassociate with a message that is poorly worded or comes off as accusatory. Other groups might have a harder time getting beyond a communication that is misinterpreted.

Training workers of all ages in the skills that best address the needs of the organization will help organizations keep employees of all generations on equal footing. Orientations that introduce employees to organizational norms and expectations help set the tone for new and existing employees. A workplace culture should be established where employees are open to receiving feedback, feel comfortable asserting themselves, and can seek open dialogue with coworkers. It is up to managers to set the tone for this environment. The sensitive and diverse nature of each generation will be one that managers need to actively understand when trying to communicate in the workplace.

POINTS TO REMEMBER

- Use multiple techniques and modes of communication; take advantage of technology, but respect employees' personal boundaries and time.

- Use a common language when communicating: define terms, acronyms, or any other unique language to your employees.
- Understand that communication can be incorrectly interpreted based on individual background and training.
- Use technology as a means to receive feedback and other employee input (surveys or anonymous comments).
- Understand the difference between formal and informal communication, and make it clear which form is acceptable within the organization.

5

Career Development for Next Generation

This chapter explores the stereotype that younger generations have shorter work commitments. This notion contrasts with the idea that job duration is closely linked to stage of life the employee is currently in. Research by Cotton and Tuttle (1986) found that the following are all related to employee turnover: perception of job alternatives, presence of a union, job satisfaction, salary/wages, satisfaction with work in general, satisfaction with supervisor, the organization's commitment to the employee, the employee's age, length of time on the job, employee level of education, and the number of dependents the employee has.

The National Commission on the Public Service (2003) reported that federal civil service was losing high-quality workers due to the declining relative pay and prestige of government service. This trend has trickled down to the state level. State governments are finding the recruitment and retention of qualified workers to be of the utmost importance. The time that individuals spend with an organization is generally a strong predictor of turnover. Generational researchers suggest younger generations are approaching work differently and the employee-employer bond appears to be nonexistent with them (Lancaster and Stillman 2002). If time and tenure with an organization no longer translate into a sense of loyalty for younger workers, this may result in higher levels of turnover. Younger generations are notoriously profiled as uncommitted to organizations and employers (Lancaster and Stillman 2002). The idea that individuals would be committed to a particular job is no longer commonplace in young workers' minds.

Young workers are considered more committed to their professions and careers than to any one agency (Mitchell 2000). However, the public sector could be a place where we see organizational and job commitment based on the concept of public service motivation. Chapter 9 discusses how generation affiliation can be associated with an individual's interest to serve the public. Lewis (1991) found the federal service quit rates were higher among those who had been in the federal service for between ten and twenty years. The idea that younger workers enter public service, obtain training, and then exit was found not to be the case.

Past studies failed to separate the idea of age from tenure in a position. It is important to see how age might influence a person's decision to stay at a particular job. Moynihan and Landuyt (2008) suggested that age, experience, and geographical stability should be considered as unrelated control variables. These variables can be key indicators as to why some employees have reached a point in their life where they would be interested in maintaining the status quo rather than making a change.

Another reason that job-changing behavior should be explored in the public sector is that tremendous amounts of resources go into establishing human resource policies that focus on recruitment and retention. Costs are incurred every time an organization loses a qualified worker. Since turnover imposes costs to the organization with regards to training and institutional memory loss and can be related negatively to performance (Meier and Hicklin 2008), it is important for managers to know the needs of individuals. Research that helps explain the behavior of individuals based on their current life stage can help organizations accommodate the particular needs of their employees.

JOB DURATION AND LIFESTYLE STABILITY CYCLE

Job duration is based on three major factors that stem from research in psychology, sociology, and economics. Individual characteristics, work-related factors, and the state of certain economic variables will all influence the time an individual will spend in their job. With current literature that focuses on reasons why individuals leave jobs, job durations are explored. Beyond applying traditional turnover literature to job duration, the concept of generational differences is also included. Are there generational differences in the times that individuals hold previous jobs? Are there generational differences in the times that individuals hold previous jobs and reasons for accepting current positions?

Important terms of interest in this study include the concept of generational cohorts versus the life cycle of stability. The life cycle of stability concept suggests that generations really don't matter but rather that each generation will act a certain way based on when they are observed. In the life cycle of stability model, Traditionalists only appear to prefer long-term jobs because they are at a point in their life where job hopping is not desirable. Because of these competing explanations, it is important to examine if there is any reason to continue to give attention to this notion of generational differences in the workplace.

TURNOVER

While there is a wealth of literature that focuses on turnover in the private sector, there is very little literature on turnover in the public sector. Research on public sector turnover has increasingly found mixed results (Meier and Hicklin 2008; Moynihan and Pandey 2008). A few research projects are focused directly on state government turnover (Moynihan and Landuyt 2008; Smith 1979). This chapter will help to inform organizational leaders of specific personal characteristics that explain the amount of time individuals spend in particular jobs. Turnover is costly to any organization and should be an area to which managers pay attention.

The supply and demand of labor will ultimately influence the institutional and cultural factors that determine why jobs end. Individual qualities and a firm's needs must match up for the employment opportunity to take place. It is also important that cultural and institutional factors make work environments conducive for all types of individuals. Studies have found in the United States that lifetime jobs (defined as jobs lasting twenty years or longer) are important features of our workplace, and men typically have jobs lasting longer than women (Hall 1982; Ureta 1992). From 1973 to 1993, the number of lifetime jobs in the United States did not decrease overall. However, for less educated workers, job stability did decline (Farber 1998).

Life course/cycle research suggests that, just by the mere function of age, older generations will have longer job durations. Those generations have lived longer, and, by default, they will have had more time to be in the workforce. By looking at some frequently hypothesized predictors of job changing, this chapter explores how generation can influence work mobility and reasons for job change. This chapter also seeks to advance the managerial understanding that encompasses turnover. The life cycle of stability hypothesis asserts that individuals who are older and have considerable experience with an organization will be reluctant to change jobs (Moynihan and Landuyt 2008).

Traditional thought on women and turnover suggests that women are more likely to quit, but due to the changing work dynamics of women, this may not be the case. There is an overall new generation of individuals entering the workforce, and the changing pattern of gender in the labor force should not be ignored. Moynihan and Landuyt (2008) found that women are more likely to report quitting their jobs. However, this could be due to the fact that in the public sector, female employees may have certain advantages compared to their private sector counterparts.

Turnover can generally be influenced by three factors: environmental/economic, individual, and organizational (Mobley et al. 1979; Selden and Moynihan 2000). This chapter examines individual features and individual perceptions of work characteristics that should help inform individual job-changing behavior. Several individual and job-related characteristics are explored to help set up a foundation as to why employees decide to leave or stay with an organization.

When looking at why an individual would change his job, basic turnover literature provides a good foundation. Researchers Porter and Steers (1973) have stated that when an employee's expectations are met on the job, they are less likely to quit. Pay, participation in primary groups, communication, and centralization are four major turnover determinants (Price 1975). An employee's perception of the ease of movement within the organization is another factor that will influence job duration (March and Simon 1958). Job satisfaction has historically been the most significant predictor of turnover (Cotton and Tuttle 1986; Mobley 1977; Mor Barak, Nissly, and Levin 2001). These ideas may seem old or outdated, but it should be noted that many of these issues still play a large part in turnover.

Research on turnover, however, has ignored many aspects of job movement. The ease of movement from job to job can be a function of economic conditions. At times when jobs in particular sectors are limited, there may be longer job durations not because of high job satisfaction but more as a result of limited opportunities. Three economic variables that influence turnover include the state of the labor market, the sector of activity, and the geographical location of the organization (Pettman 1975). Studies on employee turnover have also historically looked at turnover as an endpoint (Price 1976, 1977). This chapter extends this debate by looking not only at job duration but also at the next step, which is turnover. Turnover has consequences for the individual, the organization (social and economic), and society (Muchinsky and Morrow 1980). Many organizations experience interfirm movement. Job switching may take place, but that movement may be within the same organization. Individuals who want particular types of benefits out of their current jobs may switch within their firms rather than change organizations.

Several individual characteristics can help explain the ease with which an individual would be able to change jobs and organizations: gender and minority status, familial constraints on job movement, role as primary household earner and household size, length and time in position, and educational level. When these individual characteristics are not analyzed separately but rather are examined as intersecting human capital characteristics, the life-cycle hypothesis is collectively proposed. Theory should look at not only the collective aspects of an individual's life but also the external conditions that may help shape attitudes toward work. Generations share common history and experiences that could influence how they will approach certain life cycles. Moynihan and Landuyt (2008) found support for the life-cycle stability hypothesis. They define this premise as recognizing employees who reach a certain measure of stability in their life and who have pressing economic and familial concerns. They are less likely to seek the changes brought about by seeking a new job. Their finding is consistent with a human capital view that employees develop organization-specific capabilities that make it difficult for them to switch firms, but it is also consistent with a general reluctance to pursue change, as suggested by the significant results for the other life-cycle stability variables.

Separate job characteristics like seniority and tenure within organizations generally produce individuals who are less likely to quit and change their jobs (Lewis and Park 1989; Mor Barak, Nissly, and Levin 2001). When looking at public organizations and job-changing behavior, previous affiliation with the organization may be a key to an individual's behavior regardless of age. Civil service practices may mitigate traditional job-changing behavior in the public sector.

Time of service with an organization can help explain why individuals stay with their particular job because firms and employees invest jointly in firm-specific human capital (Becker 1962). It should be more difficult for both the firm and the worker to end their relationship the longer they are together. Many state governments apply pension penalties when individuals leave, so length of employment could be negatively related to job changing (Ippolito 1987). Generational and age differences could come into play when thinking about pension penalties. Younger workers, who are further away from retirement, may not be as focused on such penalties and thus may be more likely to change jobs.

WOMEN AND EDUCATION: CHANGES WITH
TIME AND GENERATION

Much like accounting for age and time with an organization, women and minority status have been included in most conversations about job change. As a result of traditional constraints in the workforce for both groups, they have been considered to be more likely to quit. Recent research has shown that women and minorities are either less likely to report the intention to quit their job or are not statistically different from their counterparts (Kellough and Osuna 1995; Bertelli 2007; Lee and Whitford 2008).

Moynihan and Landuyt (2008) found that women are significantly less likely to state an intention to quit their job. This finding aligns well with generational studies because it could be a reflection of the changing nature of women's work over time as well as a reflection of job opportunities provided to women in the public sector. Due to the changing nature of gender and labor force dynamics, there could be a relationship between generational cohort affiliation and job duration. The original assumption that women would be more likely to leave is based on the idea of a single breadwinner household and a woman entering and exiting the workforce as she saw fit. Women are not only increasing their numbers in the labor force, but they are also more likely to have a larger share of household earnings. While women may be more likely to quit work, this handbook suggests that they will still have overall longer job durations. Women's roles are changing in the workforce and society, and this could be reflected in how younger generations view work. The idea that women were more likely to quit might not necessarily have been a function of gender but rather because of their wage-earning role in the family.

Family situations also can affect an individual's decision to change jobs. There are risks associated with finding a new job. Heads of households and employees from larger households are generally less likely to leave a stable job (Blau and Khan 1981). Although Mor Barak, Nissly, and Levin (2001) found that this is not always true, it is still expected that individuals who are married and have children will have longer job durations. Education is also an individual characteristic that should be considered when looking at job durations. Education provides opportunities and should increase the ease of movement from job to job.

ORGANIZATIONAL COMMITMENT

Organizational culture includes job characteristics, Human Resource Management (HRM) practices, and work environment. When looking at job duration, job characteristics such as workload, job satisfaction, and status can determine if an individual is more or less likely to remain in a particular position. Individuals who are least likely to leave their current position are those who are more satisfied with their jobs (Cotton and Tuttle 1986; Mobley 1977; Mor Barak, Nissly, and Levin 2001). In the private sector, there is literature that suggests that individuals who hold higher positions are more likely to leave their jobs (Cotton and Tuttle 1986). While this could be based on greater opportunity to move, there is not much literature in the public sector to support this claim. Lewis (1991) found that more senior federal employees are less likely to quit their jobs.

Certain HRM policies can mitigate an individual's duration in particular positions. While the data does not allow testing of the direct effects of state-level human resource policies, types of policies the respondent is looking for are included in the data. By looking at an individual's motivation for accepting his current position, duration in previous jobs could be related to the lack of particular policies (training, family-friendly policies, work-life balance, etc.). Many scholars believe that policies should be designed to reduce turnover (Arthur 1994; Mobley 1977; Selden and Moynihan 2000). The data report how important certain policies are to individuals when accepting their current positions.

Moynihan and Pandey (2008) found that strong interorganizational networks characterized by good relations with staff and a sense of obligation toward other staff make it more likely for employees to stay with their organization. Furthermore, they found that strong person-organization (P-O) fit, with regard to value congruence, is more likely to produce a long-term commitment with the organization. The public sector should provide a relational aspect due to a work environment that requires the giving of oneself and the emotional support from coworkers and other employees (Parker 2002).

The culture of the organization is also an important reason why individuals may change jobs. Along with other HRM policies, better benefits and advancement opportunities lower the likelihood of an employee's turnover intention (Kellough and Osuna 1995; Lazear 1999; Lee and Whitford 2008; Selden and Moynihan 2000). Policies that are deemed family-friendly are found to reduce turnover intentions (Durst 1999; Selden and Moynihan 2000). Finally, training and development appear to have varying effects on individual's turnover intention. While training and development can encourage retention, it also makes employees more marketable (Ito 2003; Kim 2005).

A study conducted by Mor Barak, Nissly, and Levin (2001) found that turnover and intention to leave among child welfare employees, social workers, and other human service employees is related to burnout, job dissatisfaction, availability of employment opportunities, low organizational and professional commitment, stress, and lack of social support. Their study suggested that these variables are weakly related to the balance between work and family, but more so for organizational and job-based policies. This seems to be a false comparison because availability of employment opportunities would likely be related to an individual's human capital. Also, commitment to a profession could be related to personal characteristics. While the main antecedents to individuals changing jobs could be at the organizational level, many of those organizational connections are based on factors that would be personally related to the employee. Organizations can play a major role in promoting retention of employees, but individual characteristics should not be ignored.

GENERATIONAL DIFFERENCES AND ORGANIZATIONAL MOVEMENT

Another area where generational differences need to be explored is organizational commitment, and the reasons why individuals stay with some organizations and not others. Generational profiles suggest that older generations see job hopping negatively, so their promotions and job changes will be more likely to take place within their organization (Lancaster and Stillman 2002; Mitchell 2000). Younger cohorts, however, see job changing and changing organizations as a necessary condition to achieving a particular salary and career goals (Lancaster and Stillman 2002; Mitchell 2000). It is expected that time spent on previous jobs will be longer for individuals who come from within the organization. Employees who are highly mobile may possess certain qualities that place them in high demand, and they will therefore have shorter job durations.

Generational literature suggests that younger generations will not be as loyal to any particular organization as older workers have been (Bradford 1993; Adams 2000; Kupperschmidt 2000). It is important to note that this section is looking at time spent with an organization and not simply on a particular job. Tenure with an organization is usually a good predictor of turnover; however, this is based on a notion of loyalty from both the employee and employer. If the traditional employment bond is broken between generations, tenure may not predict such an outcome.

Another common myth or stereotype of young generations is their lack of commitment to organizations (Miniter 1997; O'Bannon 2001). Moving beyond the duration that individuals spend in particular jobs, generations can also differ in the type of job changes they make. More specifically, the likelihood that an employee's job history will only have one organization or multiple organizations based on generational affiliation. If the employee-employer bond is truly broken with younger generations, tenure within an organization will not be a strong predictor of an individual taking their next job with their previous organization. Tenure is used in industrial and organizational literature to define the number of years that someone has formally been with an organization (Trimble 2006). The relationship between tenure and organizational commitment may vary from generation to generation.

Changing work values may affect organizational values, and as one generation transitions into leadership positions, an organization will be influenced by that generation's culture (Smola and Sutton 2002). The success of human resources initiatives (Jurkiewicz 2000), corporate culture (Judge and Bretz 1994), and ethical issues (Dose 1997) can all be influenced by generations entering and leaving the workplace. The need for recruitment and retention is important to all organizations. Managers of younger generations are encouraged to pay attention to the needs and wants of that particular cohort. Younger generations will increasingly search to have a better work-life balance (Smola and Sutton 2002).

WHY DO WORKERS LEAVE?

Workers leave and change organizations for a variety of reasons. Some generation researchers have found that when comparing Generation Xers to Baby Boomers, Generation X members reported having a stronger desire to be promoted more quickly than their older counterparts (Somla and Sutton 2002). Comparing workers in 1974 to workers in 1999, Somla and Sutton reported that Generations Xers are much more of a "me" oriented generation compared to Baby Boomers. The younger generations are found to be less loyal to the company, want to be promoted more quickly, and are less likely to feel that work should be an important part of their lives. On the opposite side of these findings, Generation X members surprisingly reported that they felt they should work hard, even if their supervisor is not around; and they believe that hard work is an indication of one's worth (Somla and Sutton 2002).

Young workers entering the workforce are a source of both excitement and concern for organizations. Young workers bring energy and vigor, and, at the same time, younger generations have been labeled as having different values and motives than previous generations (Trimble 2006). It is important for managers not to attribute generational differences to attitudes and behaviors that might be a by-product of less job experience and fewer years of job tenure.

Some theories about Generation X members in the workforce suggest that job security to them will come from options rather than commitment (Mitchell 2000). Experience and seniority are not the keys to job progression, but the ability to add value—and not just mobility versus stability—should matter (Singer Group 1999). Younger generations will be most valued if they have multiple job offers and will, in essence, consider themselves "free agents" with very few long-term commitments to any one employer (Singer Group 1999). In order to retain younger workers, feedback should be swift, and broader job roles rather than specialization will be required (Singer Group 1999). This seems like a good way for younger generations to maximize their skills, which can also make them more marketable. Tenure helps predict job satisfaction in two ways: dissatisfied workers leave organizations, and job satisfaction and organizational commitment relate to one's identity (Trimble 2006).

Career stage has been found to be more important in explaining organizational commitment than generational status (Valenti 2001). But when career stage was controlled for Generation Xers, it was discovered that they were not different from older generations in their affective commitment (emotional identification with and attachment to the organization), but instead had less continuance commitment (commitment to stay with the organization because alternatives are lacking) (Valenti 2001).

Generational research has covered not only the public and private sector. Jobs associated with religion have found there is a need to explore the organizational commitment, job satisfaction, and turnover intention among the generations. A study of 468 missionaries found that tenure with the mission's organization was a stronger predictor of organizational commitment, job satisfaction, and turnover intention than was age (as defined by Generation Xers versus older generations) (Trimble 2006). Trimble also suggests that mission agencies should give greater attention to tenure rather than age and should not ignore the role that job satisfaction plays in an individual's commitment to an organization. In missionary work, it has been found that Generation X members tend to be disillusioned about the future, reject spiritual absolutes, come from dysfunctional families, and are more often driven by personal experience and emotional involvement (Trimble 2006). Employees with less than ten years of service desire clear communication, verbal encouragement, respect for their opinions, and inclusion in the decision-making process, and mentoring from their supervisors. The research on mission work, however, has

Table 5.1

10 Keys to Maintaining an Adequate Workforce

1 Redesign workforce processes and adopt technology to increase efficiency, effectiveness and employee satisfaction. Engage midlevel providers to enhance care delivery and build collaborative, multidisciplinary teams.

2 Focus on retention, including workers who have reached retirement age. One in three baby boomers is still in the workforce. Hospitals and health systems must engage older workers, allowing inclusion in decision-making and offering flexible work arrangements, among other things.

3 Attract a new generation of workers. Attracting younger generations to the health care workforce is essential to maintaining staffing levels. Younger generations are drawn to high-tech fields and seek work-life balance. Keep in mind that the recruitment of younger workers may require a shift in traditional recruiting techniques to include such social media outlets as Twitter.

4 Focus on hiring the right people. Behavior-based interviewing versus skill-based interviewing can build effective, long-term teams. Peer interviewing provides additional insight into whether a candidate may be the right person for the job.

5 Seek feedback. Conduct 30- and 90-day interviews to gauge the perception of new hires. This will enable timely action if expectations are not being met. Daily rounds also provide an opportunity to get to know what's on employees' minds.

6 Measure. Regular satisfaction or loyalty surveys help organizations stay on top of employees' needs and desires.

7 Reward and recognize. Acknowledging and rewarding employees for excellence fosters goodwill and helps establish an environment in which employees want to work.

8 Develop the workforce. Ongoing training provides employees with an opportunity to enhance their skills and enable advancement within the organization.

9 Eliminate low performers. A poor performer can add to workplace stress and create a toxic work environment, not to mention the potential impact on the quality of care. Eliminating poor performers will demonstrate the organization's commitment to quality and accountability to its employees.

10 Provide a competitive benefits package. Appropriate compensation is a must, but creativity goes a long way. Organizations can enhance benefit packages by offering on-site child care, concierge services, flex scheduling and housing allowances, among other things.

Source: Lee Ann Jarousse, "Best Practices for Recruitment & Retention," *H&HN*, April 1, 2011, http://www.hhnmag.com/display/HHN-news-article.dhtml?dcrPath=/templatedata/HF_Common/NewsArticle/data/HHN/Magazine/2011/Apr/0411HHN_FEA_gatefold (accessed December 3, 2013).

one flaw. In conducting generational research, it is important to separate the societal and social effects, which differentiate belonging to a generation from age.

Trimble seems to use generation and age interchangeably. "The mission agency worried about generational differences (that is, the effect of age) in organizational commitment, job satisfaction, and turnover intentions" (Trimble 2006, 349). There are apparently varying beliefs in true generational differences. Smith (2007) reported that Generation Xers do not plan to stay with one job or company throughout their career. While it is clear to some that the work ethic differs across generations, it could differ for good reasons. Generation X members have a broader appetite for technology and learning, which explains their need for change (Smith 2007).

POINTS TO REMEMBER

- Understand the contributing factors to your organization's turnover. If an organization knows why employees are leaving, it should begin a course to correct or lessen those issues. Some level of turnover is healthy for organizations, but at some point, it will become costly and damaging to the workflow of the organization.
- Job changing for young workers can be prevented; younger workers want to feel valued, needed, and know that they have a future. If organizations can provide some level of security to these individuals, they may be able to limit the amount of job hopping that is expected of younger workers.
- Pay attention to issues of diversity. Understanding changing demographics can help organizations plan appropriately for employee career pathways.
- Nonprofit organizations should attach career development to organizational missions. This is a great way to retain employees. Make them believe in the mission. People of all ages will work for a cause they believe in.

6

Nonprofit Leadership Succession

If a manager has the knowledge to lead Millennials in the workplace, then they are way ahead of the game. Above all else, the newest generation of workers want meaningful work; most other generations focus on high pay (Jenkins 2013). Failure to understand these differences about the core motivator between generations can present challenges in the workplace (see Figure 6.1).

Misunderstanding an employee's motivation can be a serious detriment to an organization's operations. This is also true in the academic setting. We need to find a happy medium with knowing and understanding what each group wants out of the job. Leaders must communicate with employees to understand what their needs are, and employees must feel as though they are in a safe place and can share this information without negative consequences. This is a challenge because employees may not feel that managers are receptive to their feedback. This fear and perceived lack of acceptance of personal needs is not productive for the workplace (see figure 6.2 and 6.3). When Millennials begin management positions, they will have to remember that encouraging and inviting communication is most appreciated.

When organizations lack available management resources, they are going to have to look to Millennials to fill the void. Generation X is not large enough to replace retiring Boomers. If organizations do not downsize, they will have to make sure they have appropriately groomed younger generations and engaged in leadership training. Investing in staff members who are considered to be job hoppers may seem like a risk, but it is that very investment that will encourage younger employees to commit to organizations. Younger generations of workers do not like delayed gratification, so any indication of a plan or future investment will make them happy.

Millennials possess a unique blend of attributes that are good for leadership positions. Smith (2010) found that Millennials are more likely to be attentive, transparent, passionate, accountable. They are more likely to seek relevancy, enjoy flexibility, and more likely to be concerned with work-life balance. Millennial leaders who are passionate about their work will inspire staff to be more energetic and engaged in their jobs. As leaders, they believe that respect should be earned, and they do not want to be in leadership positions without valid justification. Millennial leaders also use their need for attention

Figure 6.1   **How Millennials Describe Career Success**

Source: Ryan Jenkins, "Are You Making This Classic Leadership Mistake When Leading Millennials?" *Ryan-Jenkins.com*, September 30, 2013, http://ryan-jenkins.com/2013/09/30/are-you-making-this-classic-leadership-mistake-when-leading-millennials/ (accessed January 20, 2014).

Figure 6.2   **Best Practice: Johnson & Johnson**

Johnson & Johnson's first generational affinity group, *Millennials*, goes above and beyond race, gender and cultural diversity; it stands to foster a sense of understanding and inclusion across all generations. Its vision includes:

- **Serving as an educational resource and awareness advocate** regarding the Millennials' culture and defining characteristics
- Empowering and supporting the Millennials' professional growth and success
- Establishing relationships between Millennial employees and all other associates to **foster a deeper understanding of the Millennials' population**.

Although its namesake references those of Generation Y, *Millennials* is open to everyone, cultivating knowledge sharing among all generations. The group adds value for the Johnson & Johnson enterprise as well by providing insight into this generation of consumers. In addition, like its other Affinity Groups, Johnson & Johnson believes that *Millennials* provide leadership development opportunities and exposure that contribute strongly to retention and development of all employees.

Source: Lauren Stiller Rikleen, *Creating Tomorrow's Leaders: the Expanding Roles of Millennials in the Workplace,* Executive Briefing Series (Chestnut Hill, MA: The Boston College Center for Work & Family, September 12, 2011), www.bc.edu/content/dam/files/centers/cwf/pdf/BCCWF%20EBS-Millennials%20FINAL.pdf (accessed January 21, 2014).

as a management technique. These skills and strengths should be nurtured, and organizational mentors can use them to their advantage. Using orientation as a way to merge these skills with standard operating procedure is a good way to mesh employee skills and organizational needs.

Figure 6.3 **Best Practices: Sodexo**

Sodexo's *i-Gen* employee network group offers social media training, networking with colleagues about intergenerational workforce challenges and successes, an online *Generations in the Workplace* training, and intergenerational mentoring roundtables. Network group members can also participate in the four-part Career Management training, in which they learn about career competencies, development opportunities, career management and navigation, and how to prepare for a promotion within Sodexo.

The *Emerging Leaders* program helps employees develop strategic leadership skills. Program participants work in partnership with senior leaders on high-visibility business situations, working as a group to encourage collaboration and develop critical thinking skills within the context of the company's business model.

To help employees manage work and life, formal and informal flexible work arrangements are available to allow for modifications to schedules or where one works

Source: Lauren Stiller Rikleen, *Creating Tomorrow's Leaders: the Expanding Roles of Millennials in the Workplace,* Executive Briefing Series (Chestnut Hill, MA: The Boston College Center for Work & Family, September 12, 2011), www.bc.edu/content/dam/files/centers/cwf/pdf/BCCWF%20EBS-Millennials%20FINAL.pdf (accessed January 21, 2014).

GROWTH IN EMPLOYMENT

The U.S. Bureau of Labor Statistics (2010) suggest that as federal, state, and local governments try to balance budgets and reduce deficits, employment levels may change. Federal employment is likely to decline, while state and local government staff is projected to increase. Much of this employment growth will happen with new workers joining the workforce or workers having to change careers based on the recession. Either type of worker should be welcomed in the public workforce (Gothard and Austin 2010).

Nonprofit organizations are in a special situation when it comes to executive leadership succession. The nonprofit industry has to come to grips with the reality that, much like government employment, it has an aging leadership workforce. Executive directors should take the lead in managing this change. Many directors who are also founders should have a deeper interest in ensuring that the torch is passed. Career directors should also understand the role their transition plays in moving the organization into the next phase of its development. Being able to talk openly and honestly about transition plans is necessary. Organizations should be given time to prepare while employees should understand that disclosing retirement and turnover intention can be beneficial to both parties.

Nonprofit organizations can have various types of leadership succession. Organizations can execute "relay succession," which is when they pass the torch of senior management to an insider who has been identified and groomed for the position. They can also execute "non-relay succession," which happens after a competitive process with internal candidates. Organizations can execute outside succession when they bring in an external candidate. Finally, a very common type of succession and management plan includes "boomerang" hiring, where the organization brings back previous successors.

This common method of staffing occurs in organizations that have not properly managed for their next stage in succession.

MOVEMENT WITHIN AN ORGANIZATION

From an organizational and management perspective, individual movement within a nonprofit organization is often moderated by the performance of an organization. Employment that provides workers with the best potential for sustained wage growth, benefits, and a feeling of employment security is generally related to "long-term" jobs or jobs lasting at least ten years (Mishel, Bernstein, and Schmitt 2001).

Organizational theory research offers several viewpoints on the subject of managerial succession in nonprofits. Understanding managers at various levels of the hierarchy may help provide background as to why some managers stay with nonprofit organizations while others leave. The inertial view argues that organizations, particularly large ones, tend to resist change and are likely to hire from the inside even when performance is poor (Boeker and Goodstein 1993; Miller 1991). Outside succession is more likely to upset the prevailing norms and strategies of the organization and be potentially threatening to incumbents in top management because it involves greater amounts of change (Brady and Helmich 1984).

A second view of managerial succession is the adaptive view. The adaptive view suggests that organizations should change or adapt in response to environmental challenges (Friedman and Singh 1989). Managerial selection decisions represent an important adaptation opportunity. The adaptive view is the belief that when performance is poor, those doing the hiring will favor outside candidates because outsiders are perceived to be more capable than insiders of implementing strategic change in the organization (Grusky 1961; Walsh and Seward 1990). Thus, the adaptive view predicts that poor performing nonprofit organizations will adapt and recruit from outside the organization. Furthermore, during periods of good performance, an insider will be preferred because he is viewed as less likely to disrupt the ongoing organizational processes (Carroll 1984; Grusky 1961).

The final view is the contingency idea that argues that the relationship between performance and selection decisions is not direct, but rather moderated by numerous sociopolitical factors (Boeker and Goodstein 1993; Cannella and Lubatkin 1993). Cannella and Lubatkin (1993) found that poor performance by itself does not trigger an outside selection. Both the presence of an heir apparent and the incumbent's ability to influence the selection process weakened the link between performance and outside selection. Similarly, Boeker and Goodstein (1993) concluded that performance influenced successor selection. However, board composition, firm ownership, and ownership concentration influence that relationship.

There are many possibilities for movement within an organization. Organizational capacity for workers to move internally should have an influence on workers' decisions to stay or leave. Younger generations may or may not stick around to see what opportunities are available for them. If younger generational cohorts are more likely to hop between organizations, rather than within, organizational methods of promotion may be affected. Nonprofit organizations can plan for the type of succession they want to have.

WORKFORCE PLANNING

Advocates of workforce planning believe that by planning and monitoring current workforce trends and developments, human resource managers will be able to equip their nonprofit organizations with the personnel they need and prevent them from experiencing institutional memory loss as older employees retire. By forecasting for potential knowledge, skills, abilities, and other characteristics (KSAOCs), plans can be put together to anticipate the type of people that may be needed when personnel changes do occur (Pynes 2002). No level of government can ignore the retirement trend that is taking place with public employees. They must all prepare for the change in workforce and clients to be served.

More practical attitudes toward nonprofit workforce planning propose that there may really not be a need to develop long-term workforce plans. Outside of specialized positions, some managers have not had any problems filling staffing vacancies (Johnson and Brown 2004). Other agencies have proposed that since they have always been able to get by, they will be able to get by in the future. It appears that with this mentality, human resource officers are not afraid of what the future holds and therefore do not have any incentive to prepare workforce plans.

Nonprofit workforce planning has been defined in a number of ways, but for this handbook, such planning can be defined as a systematic, fully integrated organizational process that involves proactively planning ahead to avoid talent surpluses or shortages (Sullivan 2002). Simply put by the state of Washington, nonprofit workforce planning means ensuring that organizations have the "Right People, Right Jobs, Right Time" (State of Washington 2000). By planning ahead, nonprofit agencies will be staffed more efficiently and will be able to avoid panic during hiring and layoffs, which can be costly to organizations (Sullivan 2002). Organizations that prepare workforce plans can monitor external talent as well as prepare an internal talent inventory (Pynes 2002; Sullivan 2002). A successful workforce plan will allow human resource professionals to eliminate surprises, identify problems early, and avert problems (Sullivan 2002). This is advantageous to public nonprofit agencies because budgetary constraints often do not give personnel departments an unlimited amount of money to deal with extreme changes in staffing levels. Also important for public nonprofit agencies is the fact that although civil service laws have eliminated some of the difficulties in removing individuals not needing individuals, KSAOCs are not legitimate reasons. Workforce plans help limit the over-hiring of particular individuals with similar skill sets.

Workforce plans are not just sheets of paper or guides that should be completed and then placed on a shelf and ignored. These plans are active plans that must be monitored and updated. They will generally include forecasting, succession planning, leadership development, recruiting, retention, retirement analysis, identifying job and competency needs, and some type of environmental forecasts (Sullivan 2002). Most important to the public is the need for good recruitment and retention strategies. Human resource professionals are beginning to promote state employment as an employer of choice, and by doing so, they are improving recruitment and retention efforts of talented employees (Scott 2004). While all of the moving parts may seem intensive and time-consuming, the benefits of reduced labor costs and eliminating the likelihood of personnel surprises are priceless to nonprofit organizations (Sullivan 2002).

As the workforce continues to age, nonprofit agencies need to be aware of the irreplaceable knowledge, experience, and wisdom that will be lost when certain individuals leave the organization (Boath and Smith 2004). Plans that deal with the knowledge maintenance of an organization help capture and distribute the knowledge of managers and coworkers. A way for organizations to do such maintenance is to identify the knowledge that is most at risk and institutionalize it within career-development processes (Boath and Smith 2004). Organizations must build knowledge communities that capture expert information and insights into how their business operates. Informal information transfers are just as important as standardized ways that information passes from one employee to another. Organizational knowledge loss or "brain drain" is a problem for the entire employment life cycle: recruiting, hiring, performance, retention, and retirement (Boath and Smith 2004). Nonprofits will be especially susceptible to "brain drain" as the Traditionalist and Baby Boomer organizational founders prepare to retire. They must ensure that they have passed on information in order for their organization to survive a new successor.

Some government and nonprofit officials believe that the retirement crisis is not a great cause for concern because many employees will not retire when they first are eligible. Data from a *Los Angeles Times* poll in October 1999 found that 44 percent of those polled planned to work at least part-time after they came of retirement age (Leibowitz 2004). As a means of not responding to every retirement, the Commonwealth of Pennsylvania uses a "Retirement Probability Factor" to find the occupations that will be most affected and those where it will be difficult to hire and train replacements (Anderson 2004). When dealing with a soon-to-retire workforce, management should plan effectively, identify areas needing immediate attention, and mobilize stakeholders to action (Anderson 2004). All of this evidence is even more reason for nonprofit organizations to plan ahead for the makeup of their workforce.

Some human resource professionals feel the need to plan for the worker shortage and not as much the retiring of their employees since some evidence suggests that these individuals will not retire right away (Anderson 2004; Leibowitz 2004). There is a need for workers who have knowledge and experience, and the best way for some agencies to find and identify these individuals is by looking within their own organization. The shortage exists in the younger workers that will be left to support the population of aging workers (Leibowitz 2004). Nonprofit organizations are losing knowledge and should be able to plan so that the rehiring of retired individuals will not be necessary.

The use of such career development can help both senior and junior members of organizations fulfill intrinsic and extrinsic needs, which serves as an important career motivator (Lewis and Ha 1988). Career stagnation and slowdown act as both a deterrent for individuals to enter the civil service and a catalyst for more qualified individuals to depart (Lewis and Ha 1988). Increases in educational levels throughout society make for a more educated workforce, but this does not always increase the experience levels of individuals.

Workforce planning has been an answer to many public nonprofit agencies and is receiving a tremendous amount of attention in public administration literature. A combination of the hiring boom in the 1960s and 1970s, coupled with downsizing efforts in the 1980s and 1990s, has left fewer younger employees in state government ranks when older individuals look toward retirement (Scott 2004). Many plans created by state governments to deal with the problem include more flexibility in the hiring and pay practices to give them a more competitive edge at recruiting special and talented individuals (Scott 2004). Assessing at-risk leadership qualities and civil service reform are among the top initiatives that states are engaging in. More important, states are trying to present themselves as employers of choice by improving their image (Scott 2004; Sullivan 2002). Nonprofit agencies try to increase their competitive strategies by improving pay and benefits, increasing internal flexibility, and, most important to the area of workforce planning, maintaining their organization's reputation as a desirable place to work (Nigro and Nigro 2000). Financial constraints are often blamed for government's inability to attract and retain qualified personnel when status of government employment is equally important. The images created by politicians, civic leaders, voters, and clientele groups all affect the position of government as a competitive employer (Nigro and Nigro 2000). Civil service reform has tried to address these aspects and current obstacles in addressing government's image.

Workforce planning for nonprofits has been a popular topic in the field of human resource management since the late 1990s (Johnson and Brown 2004). Many agencies realize the need to create effective workforce plans but have been faced with limited resources, and circumstances requiring more immediate attention have prevented them from beginning planning. A survey of workforce planning conducted by IPMA-HR (Johnson and Brown 2004) revealed some of the reasons nonprofit organizations have not created immediate workforce plans: it is not an immediate priority with city management, lack of time and manpower availability, budgets restrict agency from planning for the future, normal recruitment/retention efforts have been enough to get by, and some agencies do not find it difficult to fill vacant positions.

Shockingly, 63 percent of respondents did not have workforce plans. More than 39 percent of those responding to the survey did state that the workforce plan was aligned with the organizational strategic plan, and 40 percent said that the workforce plan process was aligned with the organization's budgetary process. The programs that comprised 68 percent of the strategies implemented as a result of workforce planning analysis are recruitment, retention, competencies, and reduction in force (RIF). Finally, some of the specific barriers that prevented nonprofit human resource professionals from completing workforce plans are preoccupation with short-term activities, insufficient staffing, lack of funding, lack of executive support, and restrictive merit system on hiring (Johnson and Brown 2004).

Those that responded to the survey listed some of the positive outcomes or benefits that they felt were a result of their workforce planning process: raised awareness of the mass of retirees, abilities to plan where retirements were happening, efficiencies have been found by restructuring departments, improved strategic plan implementation, and increased awareness to top level executives (Johnson and Brown 2004). When examining the supply side, nonprofit organizations should be aware of the general or normal attrition rate of employees (Anderson 2004). How are public managers supposed to find time to deal with the present and plan for the future?

There has been very little mention so far in the literature about the role diversity plays in nonprofit workforce planning. It is important that organizations align overall organizational goals to include those diversity initiatives that help to ensure that diversity will be a top-level function (Mathews 1998). Commitment to diversity, like workforce planning in general, is something that needs to be recognized and supported by top managers. The nonprofit workforce today is composed of more females, immigrants, minorities, and older workers, and so it is important that managers find a way to incorporate all types of workers in their workforce (Carroll and Moss 2002; Mathews 1998). Places of employment are not just different on the outside; many workplaces are made up of individuals with very diverse lifestyles: single parents, unmarried individuals with spousal equivalents, gay couples, job-sharers, two-income families, and individuals who may have disabilities (Mathews 1998). Incorporating these trends into management can be done by aligning the strategic and workforce plan to include diversity principles. The challenge for many personnel mangers is convincing decision makers and top level managers that it is important to recognize demographic, global, and economic forecasts of the workforce into the strategic plans and goals of the organization (Mathews 1998).

Diversity gives nonprofit organizations a number of key benefits. Broader knowledge, skills and abilities, decisions based on different perspectives, and better service delivery to diverse populations are just a few of the added benefits that organizations that manage diversity receive (Mathews 1998). Many nonprofits still see large gaps in the numbers of women and minorities in top management positions, which should be addressed during diversity analysis (Wolf et al. 1987). Workforce planning identifies the organizational objectives and human resources role in meeting those objectives, so diversity should be considered somewhere in the discussion. Since nonprofit agencies are not growing as fast as they once were, the opportunities to recruit and promote women and minorities will become fewer and fewer, so organizations need to plan for these changes now (Wolf et al. 1987).

Identifying employees' skills and abilities is half the battle, and nonprofit employers should look at the social representation within the organization and determine those needs (Mathews 1998). Much like the idea of planning ahead for workforce changes, organizations should plan ahead for cultural changes as well. Workforces today are fairly stable in middle- to upper-level management, and so promotion and ways to increase representation will need to be planned for and cannot be added at the last minute (Wolf et al. 1987). Quick-fix plans do not help organizations, and they will not be any good when maintaining a public workforce. Monitoring meaningful cultural change and diversity practices should be included in workforce plans that are focused to the organization as a whole culture and not just individual employees (Mathews 1998). Diversity and workforce planning should not be separate from reaching the overall goals of the organization.

Another important aspect that has been mentioned throughout the literature is that these plans should be put into practice and not just exist as reports that are completed because they have to be (Anderson 2004; Bechet 2000; Johnson and Brown 2004). The more information that nonprofit agencies have on their staffing needs, the better prepared they will be when planning for the future. The idea is that agencies should start before the crisis happens. Many of the agencies that just got by in the past may be faced with hardships in the future that they are not prepared for.

All nonprofit organizations must be engaged and committed to organizational succession. Organizational planning should be aligned with strategic plans and implemented in the same way, that is, these plans should not just be pieces of paper but should be actual documents that are tied into day-to-day organizational functions. Organizational culture must be adaptable to any form of succession planning. Grooming the next generation of employees is a great way to focus on planning. Monitoring organizational turnover can give mangers an idea of what they may be doing right or wrong in managing different generations of workers. Most important, any sort of transition planning should be connected to the nonprofit's mission and values. This is highly relevant for nonprofit organizations, which should include the mission in every management decision they make. Only by doing this will they ensure that they are acting in accordance with the core purpose of the organization. Executive directors must be able to understand the climate in which they are operating and plan accordingly. Transition can take place for a number of reasons, and it can be a smooth process.

Nonprofit organizations are experiencing increased turnover because of retiring Baby Boomers and the need for qualified individuals to fill these positions. The next generation of workers provides an ideal pool of candidates—especially if they are working for organizations that align with their purpose and personal mission.

CAREER DEVELOPMENT AND NONPROFITS

Nonprofit organizations often find that their staffs and prospective employees are motivated to join the organization because they want to make a difference in the world. Job satisfaction is greatly enhanced by professional and career development opportunities. Many organizations that make talent and leadership development a priority find that they are more sustainable over longer periods of time (Colorado Nonprofit Association n.d.) Having exposure via volunteer opportunities in nonprofits can be an important recruitment tool. Clear career advancement is where nonprofits can be competitive in retaining employees. When studying Colorado nonprofit organizations, it was found that 64 percent of employees surveyed did not feel advancement opportunities were available (Colorado Nonprofit Association n.d.).

Millennials may switch jobs often in their early years in their efforts to find a job that is the right fit for them. Since this is an "option-oriented" generation, they will seek out the right work environment. They want jobs that can help make the world a better place, and they want to feel as if they are giving back. Finding the right work environment for Millennials is a job for both employee and employer. While catering to any particular group of individuals may be time-consuming and overwhelming for employers, ensuring a full pipeline of future employees and making a positive work environment for growth is worth the effort. Organizations that are committed to social causes will have a built-in retention mechanism for younger employees. Nonprofits should really market their missions and causes to recruit and retain employees. Millennials want to make the world better, but they want their places of employment to be involved as well. Places of employment can be involved in passive and active engagement paradigms (Cone Inc. and AMP Agency 2006). Passive engagement is simply posting philosophies or mission statements in the company's intranet, newsletters, and senior leadership communications. Active engagement is actual participation in volunteer activities. These programs not only are encouraging for employees but also can be great morale building tools for the organization as well.

POINTS TO REMEMBER

- Align with an organizational strategic plan: long-term workforce planning has to align with the larger strategic missions of the organization. These plans should be cohesive and executed seamlessly.
- Identify replacements and groom them for the succession (internal or external).
- Treat succession as a priority: don't wait until it is too late to plan for executive turnover. Nonprofit organizations should never put all of their leadership hopes in one basket!
- Align the workforce plan with the organizational mission. Along with strategic plan alignment, find out how the organizational mission plays into planning. Understanding how the organization plans to grow can ensure that the right people are in place at the right time.
- Plan but be prepared for external shocks: emergencies can happen; having some organizational capacity to deal with changes will help the workforce cope in times of crisis.
- Highlight and target the next generation of leaders and ensure retention during times of turnover.

7

Undergraduate and Graduate Public Administration Education for the Next Generation

What if the concept of public responsibility didn't matter? What if nobody cared about the unique nature of public and nonprofit organizations? What if jobs were just jobs? These are just a few questions to think about when determining which direction public administration education is moving in.

This chapter is not stating that public or personal service motivation only exists in certain groups but rather that even in public administration education, there is a changing landscape of expectations and values coming into our masters of public administration (MPA) programs. It also proposes that the antecedents of public service motivation are not as strongly associated with younger workers entering the workplace. Furthermore, the traditional benefits associated with public sector work that attracted individuals to serve the public do not really exist as they did in the past. Public service was based upon a contract of reciprocity. Giving service with the expectations of some special bonuses and job security was part of the deal. So what is attracting this next generation of public service workers, and how will public administration programs respond to these needs appropriately?

When I ask students what public administration education means, they often respond: "a business degree for government or how to manage government work." What is interesting is that the span and scope of public administration programs extend much further beyond government work, and students see, when they complete their studies of public and nonprofit administration, that their options are limitless. As the nature of public work changes, so does the preparation for those who will be working in the public sector. Issues such as bureaucracy, leadership, networks, contracting, ethics, privatization, and budgeting systems are some of the topics and themes that MPA programs must be prepared to deal with in new and exciting ways.

Some concerns that currently plague MPA programs include lack of funding and resources. As grants become harder to find in the humanities, and in times of budget uncertainty, many programs are scrambling for alternative funding sources. Agencies that at one time provided tuition reimbursement are rescinding parts of the employment contract that makes it harder for some individuals to access programs. Being able to recruit talented students is something that all public administration programs should be giving close attention to. Much like public work, it must become attractive to be in the field of public administration.

Younger generations of workers may find that staying in school is the best way to make use of their time in a job market that is not always ready to make space for them. Older generations may see education as a way to remain competitive in a job market that is getting smaller. Older workers may have been downsized, or they may be casualties of organization layoffs. Either way, the motivation that people bring to their programs should be understood by faculty and administrators. Classes should have a combination of both theory and practice. Students who have not been in the workforce (pre-service) will need a deeper understanding of the nature of public service work and why the bureaucracy is set up in a way that may seem cumbersome and inefficient to the untrained eye. In-service workers, or those wishing to use their MPA degrees to position themselves more favorably in the job market, will need practical skills that they can put to use immediately in the workplace. Classes should be set up and marketed in such a way that they apply to individuals with a diverse background of motivations for seeking out public administration degrees.

Budgets and increased needs for student enrollment are especially important for public universities. State budgets are constantly becoming leaner, and many programs will be forced to find multiple sources of funding to supplement decreased state support. Public administration programs must be able to justify their existence in order to remain off the lists of programs to cut. Being able to determine and justify the value of an education of public and nonprofit administration is more important than ever. Most schools will either consider elimination of public administration programs or use tight budgets for reinvention (Kerrigan 2011).

There are examples of programs justifying their existence and using tough budget times to reinvent themselves. The Evans School at the University of Washington faced a legislature that wanted to cut small professional programs. Instead of allowing the program to die, the school presented to the legislature budget models that not only justified their existence but also managed to increase the program size. Having a program that increases the use of technology and places emphasis on program performance with continuous improvement evaluation methods makes it a stronger contender for growth long term (Kerrigan 2011). Programs must be able to adapt in changing times and, at times, may have to actually fight for their right to exist. The University of Arizona suffered a similar fate when they were nearly cut from the business school in which they were housed. In both cases, the programs were able to reinvent themselves to become more attractive and accessible to prospective students. Many MPA programs that face elimination are finding new and creative ways to position themselves as essential needs to the overall education of a state workforce. It seems interesting that government entities would be out to eliminate the very programs that prepare individuals for public work.

The public sector is one of the largest employment sectors, and having workers who are knowledgeable of the unique challenges of public work is of the utmost importance. Public administration programs may find that reorganization with other schools that provide similar programs can be one means of survival. They may find that combining with public health, management, or political science programs can be a means to ensure survival. Collaboration with other schools/universities may also be a means. Programs with large numbers of pre-service students may find they can make themselves more attractive to students if they offer opportunities for their students to study with other universities or study abroad. Having unique learning opportunities can help programs attract new students, especially in times where small program details can make major differences. Students will not only be able to expand their networks, but they will also be able to have a richer and more dynamic program experience that is not limited to one location.

ONLINE EDUCATION

Online education provides many unique opportunities for MPA programs. Many schools are not simply putting complete programs fully online but are also providing a mix of both online and in-person course offerings. Some classes are even presented as hybrids, where they meet both in-class and online during the same course period. Many well-known universities are making 100 percent online programs an available option for students. Indiana University, University of North Carolina at Chapel Hill, and Rutgers University–Newark are just a few schools that are providing fully online programs. These programs offer a variety of management, public service, and policy options for students to take remotely. These programs often have nonprofit components and can provide a quality education to those who choose to pursue a degree in this manner.

Much like the cross-generational increase in social media usage, it should not be expected that only a particular generational group will be interested in online education. Many factors—including lifestyle, work demands, and location proximity to other traditional in-class programs—will determine an individual's likelihood of choosing online education. Online education expands the scope and reach of programs. This not only can attract students regardless of generation but also can expand the profile and reach of faculty. Students will be able to study with top scholars in various fields, and this could attract students to particular programs. Providing on-campus MPA students with online course options can be a way of attracting students who want a balance of multiple learning options. Faculty and staff should be properly trained in providing online courses.

UNDERGRADUATE EDUCATION

Undergraduate education serves as a way to expose students early on to the needs of public and nonprofit administration, and it prepares students going into graduate work in the field. Making public administration attractive to younger individuals can be done in a variety of ways. Being able to connect public and nonprofit administration to jobs will be critical in times when the economy is suffering and prospective job opportunities appear bleak. Students will want to know that they will be able to find work after they complete their studies.

A degree in public administration can be uniquely attractive to younger generations. Millennials are characterized as a group that wants to be of service and feel as if they are making a difference. Academic degrees in public and nonprofit administration can help them merge passion and profession. Schools should strive to make that connection when performing outreach or recruiting at high schools. It will prove beneficial for younger students to have programs where they feel they can express themselves during their formal education.

Moving beyond public education, some schools have opted to offer undergraduate degrees in public service. After President Obama was elected in 2008, he called upon citizens to give back and serve. This has been one of the most influential and energizing requests since President Kennedy asked people what they could do for their country. Individuals entering the workforce see public sector employment as a way to give back and also begin a career where they feel value and influence. Degrees in public service place emphasis on community engagement, public and nonprofit organizations, ethics, and citizen participation. These types of educational programs are not focused simply on the management of public organizations but also on their development and values that influence them (Carrizales and Bennett 2013).

Many of these public service degree programs will require students to get some sort of service learning experience. This is where the classroom meets real world application, and it should serve as a means for students to translate course topics into the work experience. It cannot be stressed enough that job placement and job creation will be important factors in the younger generations' educational focus. They are finishing school at a time when jobs may seem few and far between. At the same time, some Baby Boomers and Generation Xers will be returning to school as a means of skill improvement and resume boosting. If they experienced downsizing or layoffs, they may find themselves back in school, pursuing the same skills and experiences as younger workers. Students of all generations will seek service projects and out-of-class experiences to help merge theory and practice. Public service programs can set themselves apart by making these projects a main part of their curricula and by encouraging their faculty to include them in their course development.

The key to incorporating service learning with a public service academic degree is the fact that instruction is based on community involvement and values that accompany the service. Valuing service as an integral part of instruction, and education is a solution that would benefit many programs. Younger generations grew up hearing that "business is better and government has been associated with corruption and waste, fraud, and abuse." So framing education outside of the strict confines of earning to manage government organizations will help recruit a generation that wants to give back but may not associate government as their ideal employer. Even the federal government recognized the need to increase attention to volunteerism and service and helped pass the Edward M. Kennedy Serve America Act in 2009. This act was originally entitled the Generations Invigorating Volunteerism and Education Act and had a major goal of reauthorizing and expanding the AmeriCorps program. Focusing on programs that expand opportunities to volunteer and foster community engagement are just the kinds of programs undergraduate education in public service and public administration try to infuse into their curriculums. There could be unique opportunities for funding and grants depending on the type of issues programs decide to work on.

Examples of values often associated with public service education include accountability, integrity, equity, efficiency, and fairness. These are also the values associated with Millennials and their generation's profile. It is not a coincidence that this next generation will be uniquely aligned with the same values that will be prominent in these programs. One of the challenges to this type of education is getting students to think broadly about a topic that may not have been an issue during their time in K–12 education. Students are not always prepared to think about big picture ideas and topics. Most students are accustomed to studying for specific tests and are not used to applying materials to their own experiences and needs. A simple discussion about personal passion and motivation can be difficult because students have rarely thought about how they can align their interests and customize their education to achieve their personal aspirations.

TUFTS UNIVERSITY 1+4 PROGRAM: COMBINING EDUCATION AND SERVICE

Programs that help encourage public service and citizen participation are being initiated from the university level. A bridge year is typically an overseas experience that students use to delay starting their collegiate years. When most individuals think of bridge year or gap years, they may associate them with individuals who have the means and resources to spend a year abroad. Tufts University has begun a new program (with a launch date of fall 2015) that allows incoming students of all economic backgrounds to spend a year in national or international service before fully enrolling in the university. Students will work in preselected service organizations before they begin their four-year college experience. This is the type of program that will directly appeal to a younger generation that places a high value on service and on giving back, and on not rushing their university careers. Other universities could use this program as a model for their undergraduate public administration/service programs.

The Tufts 1+4 program will help students gain new skills and knowledge, enabling them to:

- Work towards civic renewal.
- Develop as leaders.
- Collaborate across differences.
- Connect community service with their academic studies and career goals.
- Join a network of peers and mentors.
- Increase the capacity of community organizations. (Tufts University n.d.)

How will the students' experiences be integrated with their Tufts academic experience?

- An on-campus orientation and training will be conducted prior to departing for service sites.
- During the bridge year, students will maintain ongoing contact with Tufts faculty and staff, and with each other, using various social media and other technologies.
- There will be a concluding on-campus gathering for students to reflect on their experiences at the completion of the service year.
- Ongoing events and informal gatherings will be scheduled to keep the 1+4 alumni connected during their four years on campus. This will provide opportunities for sharing stories about the bridge year experience, building community among 1+4 fellows, and integrating what was learned with academic pursuits (Tufts University n.d.).

The Tufts 1+4 program is creating a community of service-minded students. These students will most likely continue a practice of service throughout their collegiate careers. This is the type of program that could also assist a university in connecting with the community. Both the university and the community benefit from having students engaged in the service organizations located in their service areas.

COMBINED BACHELORS/MPA PROGRAMS

An attractive option for universities is to offer a combined BA or BS and MPA program. Several universities allow students to obtain both degrees within five years. This is done by accepting a certain number of credits to count toward both degrees. This can be advantageous for students from a tuition standpoint. Students can save money by taking graduate credits while they are still classified as undergraduates. The undergraduate program does not have to be in public administration. It can be up to the program's discretion as to what they are willing to accept towards the MPA degree.

This is an area where making the connection to future careers is going to be critical to attracting potential students. Students should know that with their degrees, their potential careers are limitless. Work opportunities will not be limited to local, state, and federal government organizations. Nonprofits, nongovernmental organizations, think tanks, and private corporations are all potential employers for graduates with degrees in public administration. At some point, it will be necessary to replace employees as they retire, so training will be beneficial to many. Younger generations of workers were not raised in a time when the public sector was shown in the most favorable light. So expanding the scope of what areas a degree in public administration prepares someone for will likely make this degree more attractive. Public and nonprofit agencies will experience the retirements of older employees and will want employees uniquely trained in particular areas.

Younger generations will be attracted to work that makes them happy. This also plays out in the attraction to education and majors. "Karoshi" is a Japanese term that means working yourself to death. We do not have to worry about this with our younger generations, because they will only be working themselves to a happy end. Younger generations will only work like this if the work they are doing is truly inspirational, and, more than likely, it will be enjoyable, and it not feel like work. When a person's passion becomes a profession, there will be no reason to die living it. Besides being told they can be anything they want, this next generation of students will expect that their degrees and job opportunities will be customized to the life they want.

More cooperation and less competition are motives that will be present with the youngest generation. As we move toward running government more like a business, individuals may be less likely to be attracted to public service. This dog-eat-dog work environment is often unexpected when young students think about government work. It seems as though they think there are two separate cultures: a corporate culture and a government culture. This government culture is one where the perceived atmosphere is not one of competition and compulsion. The truth is that everyone is not after the same things, and not everyone possesses the same motivation for success. Many individuals are drawn to public service because of the appearance or assumption of collaboration. Imagine how disappointing it might be for an individual who is drawn to serve who gets there and realizes that it is just business as usual. What happens next? Unfortunately, public service motivation might not be enough to save all hope.

Moving from independence to interdependence is also where education and public work must go. The next group of workers will be much more likely to be team-oriented and engaged. They will believe that two heads are better than one. This will be a new dynamic, but fits the model that younger workers will want to be of service to someone. Collective opportunity is something of value, and these younger workers will prefer constant interaction.

Service learning is another area that public administration education should try to include. Service learning projects are not just community service projects that happen once every semester. These types of projects provide hands-on field experience that helps students further understand what public service is (Karl and Peat 2004). Service learning helps advance learning outcomes because it combines theory and practice. Giving students an opportunity to apply course material can be a way to increase the retention of information. Students who do not have work experience can benefit greatly by this type of learning.

It will be interesting to begin monitoring these programs of service to see if tracking students into service and administration earlier in their educational degrees has any impact on future careers or service. Younger generations may feel that their service does not need to be defined by a collegiate career in studying service. Programs should make sure that they have a holistic approach to roles and needs for public service in a community and that their curriculum is not just something for people interested in working in government agencies. Defining what service means in a fun, idealistic, and global manner will be the key to attracting students of all ages to public administration and public service programs.

POINTS TO REMEMBER

- Make programs valuable to both students and decision makers. Organization leaders will be more likely to sponsor students in programs if they know they will receive value added to their organizations.
- Seek opportunities to innovate prior to times of financial emergency. Don't wait until the program is under attack to find ways to prove value and worth to the larger higher education institution. Develop metrics and performance indicators that will allow justification for continued program offering.
- Market programs as a place where both passion and profession merge. Students want to match their educational interests with their personal passions. Having programs where students can customize course plans to what directly serves them best will be a way to recruit perspective students.
- Use educational programs as a means of community engagement. Universities can place students in programs that not only help expose students to service opportunities but also increase the university mission of community involvement.

8

Social Media and Public and Nonprofit Organizations

The use of social media as a communication platform has increased at all levels of government. Many individuals use social media as a main form of communication and for information dissemination. Beyond that, social media is a working platform for organizations. Job openings, civil service testing dates, open application periods, and other important work issues can be relayed through social media communication. Social media is not only an inexpensive way to share information but also a way to expand the reach of government organizations.

Social networking is loosely defined as the act of building social networks or relations among people who share interests and/or activities (U.S. Office of Government Ethics 2011). Any platform that provides a social network service is made up of forums that allow two groups to communicate. These groups can be individuals or larger organizations. The media platform allows each group to represent themselves online. The medium that can allow for these interactions can be web-based, but with the expansion of smart phone applications, social interaction can take place through e-mail and instant messaging. Online sites and social communities (e.g., LinkedIn, Facebook, MySpace, etc.) are sometimes incorrectly labelled as just social networks, but they provide so much more. Online communities are group-centered while social networking sites are mainly individual-centered. For the purposes of this handbook, a social network is any online platform that allows an owner to post information and a user to receive and share what is posted. This allows for interaction between users, which is critical to enjoying the benefits of using this platform. If organizations are only interested in posting information, they could use a brochure-type website for those needs. Posting is just the first part of social networking; allowing the user to engage is the added benefit of establishing online communities. Several sites and applications allow this interaction: Facebook, Twitter, Instagram, LinkedIn, and Tumblr to name a few. Other means of sharing information can include online blogs, podcasts, Google+, Pinterest, and YouTube channels, as you can see on Tables 8.1 and 8.2. In this chapter, we will discuss reasons for using social media and how organizations can choose the best platform, if any, for their needs.

Social networks can be housed internally to the organization or provided by an external or commercial host. Commercial hosts include Facebook, Twitter, and LinkedIn,

Table 8.1

Broadcasting Activities	Listening Activities	Communitarian Activities
Building brand/organizational presence	Gaining information/feedback from the media	Facilitating or enabling peer to peer communication and interaction internally in the organization
Communicating to the media	Gaining information/feedback from members or member organizations	Facilitating or enabling peer to peer communication and interaction between members
Communicating to members or member organizations	Gaining information/feedback from stakeholders or external bodies	Facilitating or enabling peer to peer communication and interaction between customers and service users
Communicating to stakeholders or external bodies	Gaining information/feedback from customers or service users	Facilitating or enabling peer to peer communication and interaction between the public and wider world
Communicating to customers or service users	Gaining information/feedback from the public and wider world	Supporting or enhancing face to face meetings or events
Communicating to the public and wider world	Online Polling or Opinion Mapping	Hosting or facilitating online meetings or events
Livecasting/webcasting		Facilitating interactive research or academic collaboration
		Hosting or facilitating Communities of Practice or Communities of Interest

Source: Cogitamus, *Current Use, Future Trends, and Opportunities in Public Sector Social Media* (NHS Federation, August 2012), www.nhsconfed.org/Documents/cogitamus_report_Aug2012.pdf (accessed February 26, 2014).

Table 8.2

Current Use, Future Trends, and Opportunities in Public Sector Social Media

	Organizational Purpose/ Outcomes	Participants
Twitter	Breaking news Story and events monitoring Instant comment and reaction Brand promotion Thematic conversations	Journalists and commentariat Think tanks/opinion formers Corporate accounts/leaders
LinkedIn	Brand promotion	Professionals and leaders
	Peer-to-peer professional networking	Corporates

	Organizational Purpose/ Outcomes	Participants
	Managed professional communities of practice and interest Polling/opinion/interactive research Gathering information/feedback	Ground level staff, stakeholders and users
Facebook	Popular profile Brand promotion Tapping into public debate/ comments Platform for multimedia outputs	Personal/individuals' profiles Campaign groups Service users
YouTube	Brand promotion Supporting live events Platform for multimedia outputs Campaigning/opinion shaping	Personal profiles and subscriptions Professionals and media organizations Broadcasters and opinion formers

Source: Cogitamus, *Current Use, Future Trends, and Opportunities in Public Sector Social Media* (NHS Federation, August 2012), www.nhsconfed.org/Documents/cogitamus_report_Aug2012.pdf (accessed February 26, 2014).

while in-house hosts would be those developed internally to promote community within the organization. These internal sites may be listed on the organization's website but may need employee identification or passwords to access. These internal social networks can help promote morale and employee engagement, which can have an added benefit to the organization.

One of the reasons government and nonprofit organizations should use social media is because it spans generational lines. In 2009, Pew Research Center found that 73 percent of American adults had a Facebook page (Lenhart et al. 2010). Half of governments surveyed by the University of Pennsylvania had Facebook or Twitter profiles (Kingsley 2010, 3). The challenge is with website management: just because the web page exists does not mean the organization is actively engaging in dialogue on its website.

The General Services Administration's (GSA) increasing use of social media is based upon the belief that by sharing ideas and information, "we will find better ways to serve the public and fulfill our mission" (U.S. General Services Administration 2014). The GSA has a mission to deliver the best value in real estate, acquisition, and technology services to the government and the American people. "GSA encourages our employees to use social media to communicate, collaborate, and exchange information in support of the agency's mission" (U.S. General Services Administration). Even on the main website, GSA administrator Dan M. Tangherlini's picture and bio includes a hyperlink to follow him on Twitter (@DanGSA). Where GSA takes it one step further is that its website includes a Social Media Navigator that provides guidelines to its employees for the most effective and appropriate use of social media.

Social networks can be used to achieve the government's mission for outreach and public affairs. The public can participate in a conversation about relevant issues using social networks. These networks have the added benefit of providing immediate interactive communication between government organizations and their citizens. Government is promoting efficiency by using this platform because those with social media coordinators can often be immediately responsive to citizens. Many social networks allow government to be collaborative, transparent, and participatory. Younger generations of employees and citizens will often expect this to be a significant method of engagement.

There are a variety of benefits to using social media. These sites are readily accessible, have very few limits with regards to space and scope, and increase response time to citizens. Start-up costs are relatively low because most of the sites are free. Costs increase when an organization has to delegate staff to maintain postings and responses. It is not a good idea to begin the process just because it is cheap. An organization must have real plans for upkeep or maintenance. Generational differences can come into play because many organizations are using social media interns as a way to maintain their communications. People of all generations look to social network sites for information on news, weather and daily updates. Younger individuals are well versed in maintaining social media connections and are great resources for this type of position. The intern gets valuable experience in communicating important information along with increased knowledge on how to find information and respond to citizen concerns. Even if they are not the ones who respond directly to questions, they do communicate with various members of the organization to get answers and feedback.

Accessibility is essential for social networks. Many of the networks mentioned earlier are not just available online. Most of them have mobile phone and tablet applications that can be used by anyone at any place. They are not limited to time or location constraints. However, if the media platform isn't going to be monitored for certain hours, a network administrator should post the days or how often they update the site. Employees and citizens are used to getting immediate responses to their concerns, so they should be told when that will not be an option. Overall, the accessibility of social media is limitless. During times of emergency, government organizations or utility companies can tell citizens the times they will be monitoring and responding on their social network sites.. For example, during Hurricane Sandy in October 2012, some of the industries involved in the recovery efforts posted the exact times that they were able to monitor their Twitter feeds in the Twitter description information and tweet this information out to their followers. This would help manage citizens' expectations and allow them to know when they could expect a response.

While there may be some positive issues with maintaining a presence on social media, there are also areas of concern. One area of concern is third-party applications that help users post information and then simultaneously share with other sites. Applications like Hootsuite allow information to be shared on Facebook, Twitter, and LinkedIn after posting in only one location. This is helpful for increasing efficiency, but, as we know with using third-party instruments, this presents security concerns. All communication sites should be properly vetted before using them.

Social media provides a unique opportunity for government to have its own media channel. Cities are able to spread important information by sharing white papers, managing public health challenges, and coordinating responses to snow alerts and other public weather emergencies. Another place that valuable media information can be posted is on YouTube. Sharing videos is a way to disseminate information and can be an immediate way to broadcast information without needing a public access channel or other paid host platforms. A government or nonprofit organization can set up a YouTube channel, and individuals can follow and comment on the content that is shared. Certain groups that electronically follow an organization can help organizations in "narrowcasting" their information and sharing it with targeted audiences.

However, much like what was discussed with the GSA, there should be conversations prior to sharing on social media. Organizations should determine what content is appropriate for sharing and delegate specific employees to manage and maintain the site. Policies pertaining to these issues can be implemented by manager's discretion, but there may be legal issues involved, depending on the kind of work each organization performs. Just as an organization would go about establishing a general media policy, social media policies and guidelines should be given serious thought before they are implemented. What we observed in a study of social media use after Hurricane Sandy was that some municipalities that were not using social media previously did so to communicate with residents in the days after the storm. These municipalities spontaneously adapted to social media to communicate, however, they might not have had time to establish clear content policies before doing so. It is important that organizations not wait until emergencies but prepare prior to posting any media content.

In order to prepare effectively for social media, organizations must have the technology needed to set up their sites. Since everyone might not be familiar with social media platforms, organizations should train employees to use these platforms properly. Technology shock can be overwhelming. When adding social media to a communication plan, staffing, management, and information technology (IT) departments should all be taken into consideration. With social media, there is a lot of technology to learn, and it can be overwhelming for employees who do not know how to use it,. Being prepared for the teaching and learning time commitment is a major challenge for organizations. Employees who are required to maintain social media sites will also need appropriate resources.

Another concern with social media is that it is often considered a social amplifier. If an organization is highly responsive and progressive when posting, they will gain more followers. Social media postings can gain traction and views based on how well users receive the information and organizations can learn from now positively (or negatively) users respond. If, however, an organization is not quick to respond to e-mails or other forms of citizen requests, social media users will react negatively to these organizations. These users may decide to share posted information and other users' reactions magnify and grow exponentially. It is important for an organization's postings to be professional and positive at all times. In an age of scandal and enhanced scrutiny, government and other organizations must take extreme caution in the delivery of information. The transparency of social media can be both a gift and a curse in information sharing.

Moving beyond social media, mobile phone and tablet applications are also ways that information can be shared with citizens and employees of all ages. The younger generations of citizens will probably be more likely to check an app or social media sta-tus before they look on a website. These same generations will be more likely to look for online methods of contact before they plan on a trip to their local city or town hall. Much like a mobile game app, these mobile government or nonprofit applications can be used to connect and disseminate media content to users. The link to the website to access fed-eral government mobile applications is http://apps.usa.gov/. Through this site, you can access applications for help with the Food and Drug Administration, government safety, U.S. Census Bureau information, and healthcare. The benefit of these applications—unlike websites—is that they are more streamlined and free of clutter since they are being viewed on a mobile device. Many websites already offer mobile viewing, which makes the information easily viewed on cell phones or smart phones and wireless tablets (see, for example, m.fema.gov as an example of a mobile website).

GOVERNMENT USE OF SOCIAL MEDIA IN EMERGENCIES

Governments can use social media in times of emergency to communicate with citizens. In addition to posting information about emergency situations, government personnel can use social media prior to emergencies to communicate warnings. As was seen after Hurricane Sandy, social media was also used to allow victims to communicate requests for assistance and help. When situations improve, public agencies can also post information about recov-ery efforts and how they plan on addressing requests for services. Citizens can post photo-graphs and share conditions in real time with the use of social media. Organizations should be careful that they don't get into the "squeaky wheel gets the grease" syndrome and only respond to those types of requests. Social media should be used as a way of updating all citizens of the progress being made and not just citizens who received help.

Metropolitan Transportation Authority Post-Hurricane Sandy

After Hurricane Sandy hit New York City, the Metropolitan Transportation Authority (MTA) began announcing through maps posted on social media outlets which areas of the subway lines would be open. Many people did not have power, but if they were able to charge cell phones, they would be able to access information from their phones. People did not have unlimited access to television or the Internet, so putting information in multiple places was necessary in order to reach the largest audience possible. In these times, the traditional map would not work, so a truncated version of the normal subway map was posted. This was done so that the routes that currently were not working did not appear as an option to viewers. Anything that made the map more user-friendly was implemented to ensure enhanced user viability.

In addition to clearer maps, e-mail and text alerts were also used to send messages to MTA customers. Working with news media outlets, the MTA shared videos and pho-tographs of the status of recovery efforts, so information was shared in multiple forms and simultaneously. This form of communication may not be directly related to genera-tional differences, but it does indicate a generational shift in the delivery of information.

New York City has also invested in infrastructure which helps change the landscape of communications. Wi-Fi connections help enhance cellular reception and service for customers, making it easier for the city to communicate with citizens. During times of emergencies, people are affected differently, even if they are located in the same area. Social media allows people to sense the effects of an emergency and the scope of damage without having to see it directly. This could be one way to buy some time with citizens and customers. Being aware of the magnitude of the damages and repairs needed helps make citizens a little more patient during the recovery period. With limited access to information, mobile data becomes a way for organizations to communicate in times of emergency and recovery.

PURPOSES OF USING SOCIAL MEDIA

Organizations may have many reasons for using social media. Generally, we think of social media as a way of communicating with those outside of the organization, but social media can be a means of internal communication as well. Some organizations require those with social media experience to make their skills available to the organization. This is a way to share information and can also allow employees to get to know one another. Everyone may not be comfortable with sharing information online, so it will be important when developing social media policies that the makeup and demographics of the organizations be taken into consideration. In addition to providing a means of internal communications, social media serves to facilitate customer service and client feedback. Depending on the type of service or product an organization provides, setting up a platform for online comments and feedback may be relatively easy to implement. Taking a comments section that may exist on the organization's website and moving it to a Twitter or Facebook account can be a way to increase the scope of disseminating and receiving information.

Online community creation is another purpose for social media. Creating forums and even online committees can be a unique way that organizations can increase public participation. Everyone may not be able to attend town hall or standing committee meetings, so having online forums provides a new mode of coming together. This can include Skype or teleconferences. One of the added benefits when using social media for this purpose can also be cost savings. Organizations can save on using building resources by conducting meetings in this way. Although there may be some initial set-up costs, saving travel time and engaging multiple groups simultaneously are added benefits of engaging social media for feedback purposes.

In addition to internal communications, customer feedback, and citizen engagement, social media can be a way to establish online learning communities and enhance professional development. In this way, we again are thinking about social media as a tool for communicating information both inside and outside the organization. Using podcasts, posting blogs, and sharing information on more professional social media websites like LinkedIn can facilitate group learning in nonconventional ways. Added benefits of conducting workshops and engaging groups this way again may be savings in costs and travel time as well as registration fees for professional conferences. There is a great deal of free information that can be shared using social media. Sending e-mails may not be the best way to share videos or interactive information. However, when individuals scroll through their Facebook or Twitter timelines, they may take the time to glance at a picture or click on a podcast of interest. Sharing information in multiple forms can help increase the likelihood that it will reach a larger audience.

GAUGING SUCCESS

Much like website monitoring, social media sites can be monitored to attempt to determine exposure gained by posting. There may not be a way to monitor daily traffic as can be done on websites, but the number of followers and responses or comments may be an indicator of the success of your social media. Monitoring these numbers can help determine the overall reach your social media information is having. Programs and third-party organizations can assist in analyzing that information. Google Analytics helps users measure the effectiveness of the information they post on social media. Some organizations may be hesitant about using time and resources to put information on social media channels, but monitoring the impact and usage of the information can be a way to make a case for social media engagement.

Just as with organizational websites, there should be opportunities for feedback when using social media. People may prefer to receive information in a variety of ways, and if the purpose of social media is to enhance citizen participation, organizations should check if citizens are actually getting involved in the process. Organizations shouldn't just stick information on the site and then expect it is reaching the appropriate community. If time, money, and other personnel resources are being used to enhance social media communities, valuing feedback and impact should be taken seriously. While the host site itself may be free, a cost-benefit analysis might help make a case for start-up development and initial resource investment. Areas to keep in mind when gauging feedback should include increasing social media traffic, the level of interaction with the desired population, new social media channels, the tracking of social media, and employee evaluations. These areas are just a few ways that groups can manage and judge the impact of their media channels. These types of surveys should take place after implementation, but it may be helpful to survey target groups prior to developing social media sites. With various classifications, there can be between five and ten social media websites organizations can choose from. Moreover, each channel may serve a different purpose, depending on goals. Citizens and customers may be able to provide valuable information in determining which sites would be best suited for use and outreach.

NONPROFIT AND CHARITABLE ORGANIZATION USAGE

In 2010, the University of Massachusetts at Dartmouth conducted a study of the largest 200 charities in the United States to determine the use, adoption, and impact of social media in these organizations (please see figure 8.1 and 8.2). The study found that many

Figure 8.1 **Familiarity with Social Media**

A. How familiar are you with the following forms of social media?

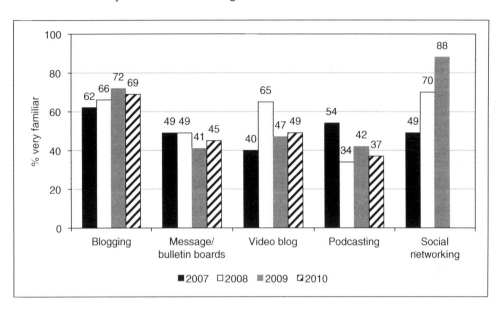

B. How familiar are you with the following social media sites?

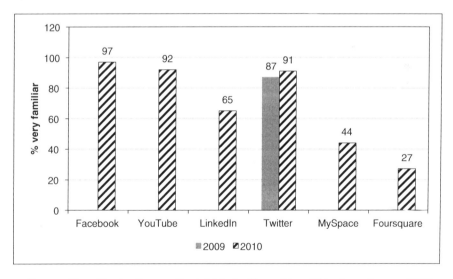

Source: Nora Ganim Barnes, *Social Media Usage Now Ubiquitous Among US Top Charities, Ahead of All Other Sectors* (University of Massachusetts–Dartmouth, 2010), www.umassd.edu/media/umassdartmouth/cmr/studiesandresearch/charity 2010.pdf (accessed February 26, 2014).

Figure 8.2 **Social Media Use and Charity Organizations**

Which of the following types of social media does your charity currently use?

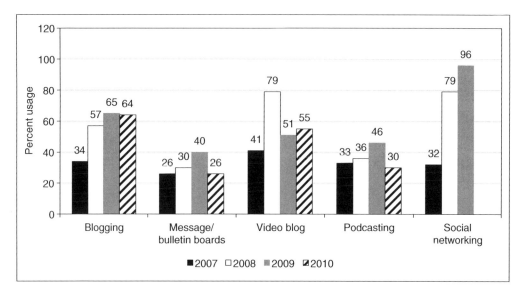

Source: Nora Ganim Barnes, Presentation, "Social Media Usage by Business, Higher Ed and Not for Profits" (Society for New Communications Research, November 4–5, 2010), http://sncr.org/sites/default/files/Nora_Barnes_SNCR_Presentation_Social_Media_Usage.pdf.

organizations find social media to be a valuable resource when trying to increase aware-ness of their mission and a helpful tool in fundraising campaigns (Barnes 2010b). For the respondents, the most common social media tools used were Facebook, Twitter, and YouTube. Many organizations were also increasing their use of blogging as a means of information sharing. When developing social media strategies, it is often important for charities and nonprofits to align such strategies closely with their marketing strategies and communication plans. This is a bit unique when thinking about traditional public sector organizations. Since the customer base for most public sector organizations is already determined by jurisdictional boundaries, the increased need to market is not inherent as it is in the private and nonprofit sectors.

Social media can be used in the nonprofit sector for various reasons, such as expand-ing an organization's mission, recruiting volunteers, raising funds, and posting posi-tions for job vacancies. It is important to make sure that the right information is being shared to achieve the desired outcome. Blogging in the area of charities and nonprofits has become a way of sharing important information, though it is not a main avenue of engagement (Barnes 2010b). Blogs may be one way to communicate, and they can help customers get a deeper understanding of the work the organization is doing. Most blogs allow for comments, and this is something that can be monitored to provide two-way communications. Using social media is a way to engage the three major resources for these charitable organizations: volunteers, donors, and employees.

In order to ensure social media success, organizations should develop a clear social media strategy. This should include marketing and communication. A social media strategic plan can be developed by an organization, just like any strategic plan. It should involve support by top management and should receive feedback from prospective users. Developing a social media vision and strategy should be done fairly quickly after deciding to use it as an option. Along with strategy and top management support, having dedicated social media staff is also going to be a key to success. Social networking is something that will need to be managed, so staff or interns will be necessary for monitoring and engaging with customers or citizens. These social media plans should be determined shortly after any organization decides to participate in social networking.

Nonprofits can also use social media as a platform for calling groups to action. Social media can be used to recruit nonfinancial participation from individuals and supporters. Spreading awareness and then asking interested parties to act is where social media can provide support to organizations. Facebook and text messaging are increasingly becoming platforms for fund-raising. Organizations should use this to their advantage. Most individuals involved in nonprofits are already using Facebook; requiring them to go to an additional website may be a deterrent to making a contribution. If supporters can take care of everything on one platform, successful participation may increase. Using social media as a fund-raising medium is also discussed in chapter 3 on volunteering.

Public and nonprofit organizations should be aware of the market and promote themselves to different generations. Sending direct mailings will not have the same appeal to Millennials as it will to Baby Boomers. Some organizations are actually able to determine the exact cost and value of each type of social media. Being able to access the value of users can be helpful in planning and deciding what kinds of resources to dedicate to social media. Much like grant writers, social media directors could get to the point where they are able to pay for themselves based on the revenue they bring in and their monetary impact on the organization. This could be part of the strategic plan discussed earlier in the chapter. Social media budgets and personnel could increase based on the amount of resources that its influence can bring in.

CITIZEN MANAGEMENT

One of the main benefits of social media is the speed and efficiency in which public organizations can share information with citizens and customers. In 2009, the Obama Administration issued a legislative memorandum mandating that the public sector should use social media as a way to engage citizens and collaborate across agencies (Falco 2011). The Office of Management of Budget memorandum suggested that social media could be one way that government could increase transparency, participation, and collaboration (Mergel 2010). This followed the push of Government 2.0, which was a term developed for the public sector's use of social media. The federal government suggested that social media could be used in three ways. Social media could be a push, pull, or networking strategy (Mergel 2010). First, the push strategy is when the social media platform is used just to get information out. Second, the pull strategy will actively engage the audience and solicit feedback from users. This might consist of soliciting feedback or opinions from citizens on new policies or implementation strategies. And finally, the networking strategy is the highest order of social media engagement, where communication is highly interactive. This is when many employees and top managers are involved in the monitoring of social media pages, and social media is considered to add value to the agency mission (see tables 8.3 and 8.4). One of the main things organizations need to ensure is that social media is incorporated into their current means of information sharing and the overall mission of the organization. Having a strategy cannot be stressed enough for any organization trying to establish a presence in social media. Every organization needs to be concerned with security threats and any area where the public can view negative information.

Any social media strategy should include overall marketing needs and initiatives to develop the appropriate audience for each organization. An organization's service and the population it serves will often determine the type of social media it uses. Some organizations may need to simply share information, while others may require comments and feedbacks pertaining to the services it provides. After mission integration and forum selection, organizations should work on communication plans that will assist in guiding users on the content and information that is appropriate to share. Any monetary or

---

Table 8.3

Social Networking Users (% of adults who use social networking sites)

	Feb/Mar 2005*	Aug 2006*	Nov/Dec 2008*	Jan 2010*	*05–10 Change*
All	5	11	27	41	*+36*
Millennial	7	51	71	75	*+68*
Gen X	7	10	38	50	*+43*
Boomer	5	4	13	30	*+25*
Silent	2	*	2	6	*+4*

*Data from surveys conducted by the Pew Research Center's Internet & American Life Project. Question wording varied from 2005 to 2008. The 2005 item was worded "Use online social or professional networking site Friendster or LinkedIn." The 2006 item was worded "Use an online social networking site like MySpace, Facebook or Friendster." The 2008 item was worded "Use a social networking site like MySpace, Facebook or LinkedIn.com"

**Question wording: Have you ever created your own profile on any social networking site?

Source: Paul Taylor and Scott Keeter (eds.), *Millennials: A Portrait of Generation Next* (Washington, DC: Pew Research Center, February 2010), 28, www.pewsocialtrends.org/files/2010/10/millennials-confident-connected-open-to-change.pdf.

Table 8.4

Millennials Make Frequent Visits to Social Networking Sites

% of social networking users who visit the site they use most often . . .

	Several times a day	Once a day	Every few days	Once a week or less
All Social Networking Users	21	23	23	34
Millennial	29	26	20	25
Gen X	19	19	24	39
Boomer	11	26	25	38

Note: Based on adults who have their own social networking profile. Silent Generation not shown because of small sample size. "Don't know/Refused" responses not shown.

Source: Paul Taylor and Scott Keeter (eds.), *Millennials: A Portrait of Generation Next* (Washington, DC: Pew Research Center, February 2010), 28, www.pewsocialtrends.org/files/2010/10/millennials-confident-connected-open-to-change.pdf.

staff support should be accounted for, and the appropriate evaluation methods should be determined at this point. Safety and security concerns should be highlighted at this time to see if and where the organization may be at risk by using social media. Just like any other strategic plan, the appropriate evaluation method should meet the desired needs. Some organizations may want to test the use of social media. Having a small group of employees or customers participate in a trial run can be one way to sample social media's usefulness prior to opening sites to the public.

It should not be assumed that only younger generations will be receiving information via social networking. Facebook's fastest growing population is with the 35 and over age group. So organizations should not think that they are only communicating with younger citizens via social media. Social media has become a form of communication for all ages, but the use of social media for news and public sector advice may be an area where public organizations can make their presence more widely known. Just because social media has been a major part of the younger generation's life span does not mean it is just for them. Organizations will need to adapt to this new form of information sharing that just so happens to be associated with younger generations.

Engagement of individuals at all levels can take place with social media. Beyond public organizations engaging with citizens and customers, politicians and decision makers also have a unique opportunity to interact with supporters. Constituent work can be redeveloped when social media is engaged. Sending a tweet as a response to a citizen's concern takes a matter of seconds and need not involve a phone call or a face-to-face meeting. When issues are not complicated, or when a constituent needs to be pointed in a particular direction, social media can be a great means of communication. Twitter can also be used like a radio station, and there can be times when politicians can conduct question-and-answer sessions or hold mini-town hall meetings on social media platforms. If there are times when politicians aren't monitoring their social media pages directly (mainly Twitter), it should be clear that the proxy understands the issues to which they will be responding. Politicians should also engage in having a social media strategic plan from the time they begin campaigning. This is a significant way in which politicians can engage audiences and also call supporters to action.

Overall, social media seeks to combine traditional means of organizing while combining advances in modern technology to help disseminate information at a more efficient pace. Anyone engaged in providing public services can benefit from using social media. It is important that information be appropriate for that platform and that there are clear plans in place before organizations move forward. Social media is not a fad, and, if anything, more platforms will come online and try to become players in the industry. Organizations should access their capacity and commitment to social media engagement and prepare for the necessary management that comes along with it. Social media is a product of one generation, but it is not limited to engagement with any one generation in particular. People of all generations are using social media as a means of communicating. Social media allows everyone's reach to extend beyond any physical boundaries, which provides exposure and access to supporters everywhere.

POINTS TO REMEMBER

- Develop a social media strategic plan that aligns with the organization's mission.
- Look to younger workers for social media internships. Social media is a way of life for younger generations. Getting them involved in blogging or posting teams should be effortless and encouraged.
- Communicate the times that social network platforms will be monitored. If sites are set up for two-way communication, make sure that people know the hours that the site will not be responding directly to posts.
- Establish social media policies prior to beginning use; have broad policies that allow for growth and expansion.
- Find your social media purpose and work from there. Every organization will not benefit from being on three or more sites. If one outlet works for your organization, go with it.
- Seek feedback and evaluate effectiveness when rolling out online communication.
- Nonprofit and charitable organizations should use social media as a way to engage employees, volunteers, and donors.

9

Changing Scope of Public Service Motivation

INTEREST TO SERVE THE PUBLIC

The public sector should be concerned with how a person's interest to serve the community can be affected by generational affiliation. This chapter does not seek to define or test the idea of public service motivation (PSM) in its entirety. However, work on PSM does inform much of the literature in understanding an individual's interest to serve the public. Individual motivators for accepting jobs will be used to identify an individual's interest in serving. Literature on PSM addresses the attitudes and beliefs that individuals in the public sector share or lean heavily on compared to individuals in the private sector. Theories on public sector values and rules stemmed from work on PSM. Much of the work on PSM has been used to prove that it actually exists (Moynihan and Pandey 2007).

Public organizations face a unique challenge in maintaining their workforces. These organizations face not only an age challenge but also an information challenge. Understanding what will draw the next generation to public employment will be necessary to ensure staffing levels. This chapter helps us understand the current conditions, what can be done to attract the next generation, and why it matters. The numbers of public employees (especially federal) approaching or near retirement age is alarming:

- According to the Census Bureau, the median age of government employees is 45.3 compared to the median age of 42.3 in the U.S. workforce as a whole.
- The average age of federal employees is even higher: 47.
- 60 percent of federal employees are over the age of 45, compared to 31 percent in the private sector (Lavigna and Flato 2014).

In recent years, theoretical development and empirical work have been used to operationalize what public interest means for employees, why they develop a strong sense of public service, and how it influences their behavior on the job (e.g., Alonso and Lewis 2001, Crewson 1997, Houston 2000, Perry 1996, 1997). Brewer, Selden, and Facer (2000) noted that PSM is important not just to motivation but also to productivity,

93

improved management practices, accountability, and trust in government, making it one of the major current topics of investigation in public administration. The appearance of PSM is not limited to the public sector. While PSM tends to be particularly high for government employees, those in the private and nonprofit sectors also exhibit PSM to varying degrees (Wittmer 1991).

Perry (2000) asserts the importance of PSM as an alternative to rational and self-interested theories of motivation that tend to focus on pecuniary rewards. PSM can also explain the shape of beliefs and behavioral outcomes. The theory argues that individual behavior is not just the product of rational self-interested choices but is rooted in normative and affective motives as well. If we only study motivation from a rational incentive-driven perspective, then we will only have a partial understanding of motivation. To fully grasp the concept, we must study social processes that shape an individual's normative beliefs and emotional understandings of the world. This should be an interesting place to include the idea of generational cohorts.

Brewer (2002) stated that public administration researchers have long believed that some individuals have a strong public service ethic that attracts them to government employment and promotes work-related attitudes and behaviors that advance the public interest. Social factors have not been completely ignored in the exploration of PSM. It has been proposed that PSM depends on how individuals are socialized via socio-historical institutions, primary parental relations, religion, observational learning, and modeling during the course of their life events, education, and professional training (Perry 2000). This could also be expanded to include the common history that generations may have experienced. Memories of downsizing may be familiar to those in the Baby Boomer generational cohort. Generation X and Generation Y may have witnessed the dislocation of parents and relatives, which could make the idea of being loyal to a particular firm foreign and less appealing (Bowen 2000). Knowing the timelines during which each cohort grew up proposes that they will share some similar reference points and attitudes when applied to work.

Life course research is a theory that can readily be applied to the study of those who work in the public sector. Research on work experience has dealt extensively with intrinsic and extrinsic rewards (Johnson 2001). The life cycle approach to understanding aging suggests that individuals will have different values and experiences throughout the aging process; consequently, young adults could be considered to have less stable values when compared to older adults (Johnson 2001). This will have an impact on the amount of public service motivation they possess. PSM should not be treated as something that remains stable throughout a person's lifetime.

The idea of public service motivation has been explored in a number of ways. Scholars have suggested that individuals go through life stages in moral development (Erikson 1980). In this context, it could be expected that younger individuals have not had time to develop the same levels of societal and moral commitment as that of older people. It would be expected that looking simply at age would make youth negatively correlated to high levels of public service motivation. It could also be expected that public service motivation would have a cyclical relationship with age. Individuals enter public service with high levels of motivation, but as they become more ingrained in the bureaucracy, public service motivation may wane (Buchanan 1974, 1975).

Research on life stages and bureaucratic burnout has set up a nice foundation for the application of generational cohorts to public service motivation. This baseline hypothesis suggests that younger generations have lower levels of interest in serving the public. Generational profiles of Baby Boomers (born 1946–1964) describe them as not being interested in job changing to increase status and recognition. It would appear that these individuals might take more time and care when they look for jobs and really align themselves with organizations that they feel they could stay with over longer periods of time. Baby Boomers with high levels of public service motivation would therefore choose the public sector and see it as a place where they could make a difference and influence society.

Members of Generation X (born 1965–1980) are described as not being as attached to the employer-employee contract and as having a higher need for recruitment and rewards. Members of this generation may not be as socially developed as older generations but are more concerned with making money and looking for career security instead of job security. The experiences of this generation would not align them with traditional values found in public service motivation. As described by Lancaster and Stillman (2000), this generation will look to put faith in themselves instead of the institutions. As a cohort, it seems that Generations X members will be more concerned with self-survival as opposed to a sense of public commitment and involvement, thereby having lower levels of public service motivation.

The 1998 General Social Survey reported that only 19 percent of individuals surveyed personally chose to work for the government or civil service over working in a private business (Mitchell 2000). When this statistic is broken down by generation, Traditionalists have the highest percentage, with 22 percent of individuals choosing to work for government, while the lowest percentage is the youngest generation at 16 percent. Social psychology has informed much of the research on job values and the aging process, which suggests that job values and the rewards obtained on the job grow more important over time (Mortimer and Lorence 1979; Lindsay and Knox 1984; Kohn and Schooler 1983). Younger generations are described as being attracted to more individualistic and autonomous work environments, which should be interesting for public organizations that are notoriously associated with red tape and other barriers to day-to-day work freedoms.

The ever-changing look of the public sector workforce presents many challenges for public managers and organizations. Many sectors of employment (public, private, and nonprofit) are facing large numbers of expected retirements from the Baby Boomer generation. This poses many institutional pressures on agencies to be able to recruit and retain a skilled and diverse workforce to address problems and issues of the future. This diverse workforce will present management challenges in issues pertaining to gender, race, ethnicity, sexual orientation, and family-friendly policies.

Age will come to the forefront of management issues because of retirement possibilities and challenges in recruitment and retention. Along with age will come the popularly presented idea that generations approach work differently, and this will pose yet another management issue. In the public sector, it is expected that certain individuals will have a higher likelihood or willingness to serve the public. It is important for managers to understand how an individual's interest to serve the public could be related to the social and institutional climate that they grew up in. Basically, are the generational differences in individuals' interests to serve the public a motivator for job acceptance? The public sector should be an interesting place to look at such differences. The idea of public service motivation proposes that individuals have a predisposition to respond to motives grounded primarily or uniquely in public institutions and organizations (Perry and Wise 1990). Many studies have further developed the work on the concept and theoretical grounding of public service motivation (e.g., Alonso and Lewis 2001; Brewer, Selden and Facer 2000; Perry 1996, 1997). Although all of these studies are important, they rarely look at the possibility of the PSM shifting over time due to historical events or conditions.

The public sector also faces many potential challenges with large numbers of employees being of retirement age. The U.S. Merit Systems Protections Board (2008) has explored what techniques should be used to attract younger generations to the federal government. It seems like this topic is on the minds of many in the public sector, but little empirical research has been done to test whether generations actually have different attitudes toward public sector work.

More than ever, the ability to attract those with an innate interest to serve the public will play a critical role in hiring and retaining qualified and skilled individuals to public sector work (Partnership for Public Service 2005). Research in China found that younger workers are more likely to want jobs with stable futures and high salaries (Ko and Han 2013). Typically, the benefit of stability and salaries with steady growth have been associated with public sector employment, but as the makeup of public sector jobs changes, what will be the attracting element? The public sector cannot just rest on public service motivation.

A national study by Universum, a global employer branding and research outfit, surveyed college students and found the following factors to be the top attractors to employment (Lavigna and Flato 2014):

1. Respect for its people—53.7 percent
2. Secure employment—52.5 percent
3. Creative and dynamic work environment—49.1 percent
4. Professional training and development—45.7 percent
5. Friendly work environment—45.6 percent
6. Leaders who will support my development—42.7 percent
7. High future earnings—42 percent
8. Leadership opportunities—40.9 percent

Government employment can encompass all of these aspects, and it is important to promote public and nonprofit employment as places of growth and learning. Younger workers want to know that they will matter in their organizations. Unfortunately, public employment no longer can ensure security, but other opportunities can make up for the lack in that area. Government organizations will be fighting an uphill battle as they try to recruit young workers into an area that is constantly being bashed by media and other outlets. Younger employees are going to want to work for model employers.

The explosion of nonprofits will also hurt the traditional recruiting reliance on PSM. Potential employees have many more options if they want to work for organizations doing public work. As publicness has expanded beyond the reach of public organizations, there is an even greater need to promote the best aspect of government work. Employees of all ages could get their "public service fix" working for nonprofit or private sector organizations.

Using targeted recruitment that specifically focuses on younger workers will be a key to getting individuals in the door. Agencies can use campus recruiting or internship programs to attract younger workers early in their careers. Younger workers will want to serve, however, there is no guarantee that they will pick government organizations as their means of doing so.

PUBLIC TO PERSONAL SERVICE MOTIVATION

Younger generations of workers want instant gratification in compensation and promotions (Hammill 2005). There may be ways for organizations to make all groups happy. Many younger workers want continuous feedback and would like immediate results. Younger workers need reassurance and encouragement to feel that they are a part of the organization. This leads to the belief that younger generations of workers may possess more personal service motivation. These groups are highly service oriented, but this may not mean that they want to work for government organizations. This is much like the attraction to public administration education. There is no guarantee that a service-oriented generation will look to institutions to provide them with their outlets for service.

Personal service motivation is the idea that people will have an urge to serve but will seek out opportunities in nontraditional ways. These service opportunities might include raising awareness for a topic through social media or donating small amounts of money to service projects. There are more opportunities for people to serve—whether it is personally or with work. Organizations will have to do a better job of marketing themselves as places where individuals can bring their service talents for employment opportunities. Governments are not always portrayed in the best light, and people may lose interest in working for those organizations that are seen as scandalous or dishonest. Individuals with an interest to serve may feel better about taking their personal talents to nonprofits or private corporations that do public work.

Government organizations are facing increased competition for highly talented individuals in all generations. It is important that they to take time to understand what makes their type of service more important than others. Using the organization mission and target population as a recruitment strategy will bring the right people with the right fit into the organization.

POINTS TO REMEMBER

- Public service motivation may look different across generations; interest to serve in government organizations will fluctuate based on generational characteristics.
- Younger workers may possess more personal service motivation, and they may want to serve, but they may do so in nontraditional outlets.
- Organizations should not rely on PSM as an attractor for employment. They should market themselves based on what is unique about them.
- Use your organizational mission to define why your organization's type of service is unique.

10

Next Generation and a New World View

Why should you care about dealing with diversity issues brought about by generational differences? You should care because they exist and they are important. Generational differences are currently observed in the approach, execution, and attitudes toward work. Managers need to be aware of and informed by these differences because when managing organizations, it is important to be enlightened about employees' needs. Employees need to be aware of the differences because they must take these differences into account when interacting with each other. Conversations and topics that may be acceptable for one generation to discuss may not be appropriate when other generations are present.

DIVERSITY

Generation Xers (aka the Baby Bust Generation due to lower birth rates from the generation that precedes them) was the first generation to break through the diversity boundaries. In the workplace, they will have a need for job security, and this is difficult at a time when older generations are not retiring at a regular pace (Marston 2007). As of 2009, their racial composition was 62 percent non-Hispanic white alone, 18 percent Hispanic, 12 percent non-Hispanic black alone, and 6 percent non-Hispanic Asian alone (MetLife 2013). This group was born during the technology boom and is more tolerant of racial and ethnic differences due to being raised during the political correctness phase of the 1990s (Hicks and Hicks 1999). Unlike the Baby Boom generation, Generation Xers were the first generation to show a lower level of employee commitment and to strive for greater work-life balance (Marston 2007). This group is more comfortable with change and strives for self-sufficiency and authenticity and will not be workaholics at the expense of sacrificing family life (Marston 2007).

Baby Boomers are in the mid- to late part of their careers, and in the next twenty-five years, the entire generation will have reached retirement age (Callanan and Greenhaus 2008). Generation Y are still developing their complete generational personality, which includes future names, which could translate into the workplace. The Non-Nuclear Family generation, the Wannabees, the Feel-Good Generation, Cyberkids, and the Searching-for-an-Identity Generation are just a few of the names proposed for this generation.

This generation is highly educated, seeks flexibility, and, like Generation X before them, seeks a balanced life (Tolbize 2008). Some characteristics that set them apart include increased confidence, less process focused, and more demanding. All of these are traits that could influence workplace behaviors and interactions. A group that seeks independence and freedom may clash with a loyal and goal-oriented generation on certain tasks and interactions in the workplace.

One of the major challenges for generational interaction in the workplace is the perceived decline of the work ethic (Jenkins 2007). This may not be a generational issue but an overall trend in the workplace. Older generations have usually perceived the generation that comes behind them as unmotivated and not as dedicated. Work ethic is not just limited to generational differences. Several factors like educational level, full-time versus part-time employment, income level, and marital status all play a part in work ethic. Family values, the presence of a career mentor, and other traits developed during a person's life contribute to work ethic as well. A challenge in the workplace is to *not* place value judgments on individuals just because they are a member of a particular generation. As mentioned in this handbook's introduction, these profiles are just that. But as with any profile, certain people will not fit exactly into the profiles, and others may have parts from all generational profiles, depending on their unique makcup.

Diversity can translate to appearance and personal dress in the workplace. Younger workers are more informal in their dress even when it comes to the workplace (Twenge and Campbell 2008). One of the reasons Google is rated as a top five employer for younger employees is because of their daily casual dress code. While a relaxed dress code might not work for all organizations, employers should be aware that they may have to communicate this to their workforce. Taking things for granted could precipitate generational conflict. Employers should communicate their expectations in all areas of work. Employee orientation should become a universal part of the employment experience and should be standardized throughout an organization. It may not be the best idea to have younger employees introducing young workers into an organization because they may pass on traits and assumptions that might not be in line with the organization overall. Understanding deeper generational differences will be advantageous to organizations and managers. Something as simple as understanding the employee dress code may help workers of all generations coexist.

CURRENT CONDITION OF JOBS

Since 2000, employers have been reluctant to add jobs (Leonhardt 2013). This presents a problem for younger workers who, even in the midst of a recovering economy, are having a hard time entering the job market. Older workers who have been in the job market are trying to hold on in an economy where retirement does not appear to be a smooth financial option as they once may have hoped. Education is one area where younger workers excel, but this has done little for them in a changing skills market. It may be in the best interest for organizations to provide training for the specific skills which they will have a need for. Some of the most educated people face lower levels of unemployment because traditional education is not the only solution to the younger worker employment problem. Job counseling and job placement programs could be helpful in solving both employee and employer needs. Regions where workers are counseled saw greater levels of employment (Leonhardt 2013).

Employees are still looking for greater work-life balance, and at the same time, worker programs that promote balance are not on the rise. As a result, employment of women is slipping a bit. Programs like parental leave and part-time work once were quickly expanding and now have currently stalled in the United States (Leonhardt 2013). Younger generations possess some of the best qualities to deal with slumps in job growth. Their resilience will be necessary to deal with limited job prospects and current economic trends. Younger generations are observed to have higher levels of self-esteem and narcissism (Twenge and Campbell 2008).

There is hope that the latest generation will once again return to the Greatest Generation, mirroring those born during World War II who have more group orientation and are more dutiful and less individualistic (Howe and Strauss 2000). So employers should not count the younger generations out. What may look like apathy and lack of motivation may just be a different way of behaving. Respecting and understanding others' differences will be a critical part to a cohesive workplace. For the right organizations, it could be beneficial to accommodate differences rather than work against them. Organizations with large numbers of younger employees may find it necessary to embrace younger employees' attitudes about work and structure. Not to count young employees out, Millennials are said to be the first socially active generation since the 1960s (Ryan 2000). This is already evident in the success that we have seen in the election of President Obama and the impact that young voters had on his campaign. Many young workers flocked to government work as a result, answering a call to serve.

POLICY IMPLICATIONS

The results of each generational analysis suggest some implications for public management and personnel policy. First, it might be unwise to profile younger generations as chronic job hoppers and less committed to organizations. When managers make assumptions about younger workers based on their generation profiles, they may lose out on valuable assets. It may be the case that younger employees are less likely to spend their entire careers with one organization, but recruitment and retention efforts may help mediate their likelihood to switch organizations.

Job characteristics were found to influence employee turnover (Mobley et al. 1979). The idea that younger generations are less committed to organizations does not appear to be the case. There seems to be support for the life cycle of stability due to a positive relationship between age and job duration. The age effect once again appears to be the driving factor behind work behaviors. The opportunities for advancement associated with education should not be ignored. The correlation between generation and education should be explored. In terms of education levels, younger generations (Generation Y and Millennials) are expected to meet or surpass the Baby Boomer generation, who are the best educated generation so far (as measured by percent of people with bachelor's degree or more) (Mitchell 2000).

It is important for employers to understand what employees want out of their next job opportunity. Opportunity for advancement within the current organization seems to be negatively associated with longer job hours. As the public sector has individuals working longer, it may make younger workers more likely to have shorter job durations when they do not see opportunities for advancement (See Table 10.1).

Table 10.1

What You Can Do Right Now!

Hold discussion groups to discuss the findings in this report	Sharing your reaction to this report, mutual talent development challenges, and opportunities within your organization and community will help you prioritize needs.
Assess your community's talent development practices	Understanding the career continuum from education to retirement for any field is not easy. However, organizations should examine their current practices in the context of the larger community. Are you reaching the best applicants for your job openings? How might service learning programs at local schools help you develop the future talent pool?
Engage your board and executives in talent development planning	Enhance understanding of the roles executive directors and boards play in staff lives and careers. What does this imply in terms of budget, training, recognition, retention, leadership development, and transition management?
Commitment to diversity in hiring and staff retention	Nonprofit staff and programs should reflect the community they serve, but this requires time and effort. Explore your strengths and weaknesses in attracting diverse staff, and before you hire, think about how to make your organizational culture truly inclusive.
Make goals and measure progress	Creating talent development goals and providing resources to meet those goals demonstrates that an organization invests in and values its staff. Measure the progress in meeting objectives and build long-term plans that use the full potential of each individual. This process can help connect the dots between job satisfaction, organizational effectiveness, and impact.
Invest in staff at all levels	Avoid focusing solely on top-level management. Investing in lower-level staff can strengthen your organization from the bottom up, provide greater job satisfaction for those staff and build the next generation of nonprofit leaders.
Train, Coach and Mentor	We highlighted the link between training, coaching, and mentoring and strong organizations in this report, and organizations should work to continue basic talent development practices. While many of the outcomes of the suggestions here are long-term, nonprofits should work with their current staff immediately to see what support they need. Creating a talent development budget and plotting activities for the rest of the year will help you craft the future.

Source: Colorado Nonprofit Association, "Talent Development Initiative: Path with a Heart," 2012, www.coloradononprofits.org/training-events/talent-development-initiative/ (accessed December 3, 2013).

CLOSING THOUGHTS ON MILLENNIALS

Dealing with this latest generation of individuals in the workplace presents a few unique challenges. While the group is large in numbers like the Baby Boomers, due to their young age and prolonged educational aspirations, they have not quite challenged the workplace and infiltrated it. However, a generation that is accustomed to choices and instant feedback will present challenges for managers who are not aware of their differences. As consumers, they are used to having their needs and concerns taken into consideration and will have those same expectations when they enter educational settings and the workplace.

Being raised with unlimited accessibility to information can be one of the reasons this generation is more engaged and involved (Cone Inc., and AMP Agency 2006). The world is a very large place to this group and is not limited to their immediate location. Witnessing national and international disasters at a young age increased Millennials' worldview, scope, and concept of social involvement. Almost 16 million Millennials are considered "doers," or individuals who volunteer once a week (Cone Inc., and AMP Agency 2006). Appealing to this section of Millennials is important for organizations because this group is hardwired to serve. Somewhat like individuals with public service motivation, this group is going to be attracted to opportunities to serve. They will also be more likely to spend money that supports causes that they believe in.

CONCLUSION

Overall, Millennials and older generations want similar things out of life. Most people value family and connections with other people. Organizations and communities should explore enhancing common bonds and focus on similarities as opposed to differences. Nearly all generations have the same level of individuals who are happy with their lives overall (Taylor and Keeter 2010).

Millennials are less likely to have full-time work. This can be a function of age but also a reality of the current conditions of the workforce. Getting loyalty from these individuals is going to present a challenge because they did not receive loyalty at the beginning of their careers. Younger workers will approach a job with a free-agent work mentality. Even after obtaining employment, they will more than likely still keep an eye out for other job opportunities.

As adults, Millennials are more tolerant of different values and lifestyles within society than the generations that precede them. This will also manifest in the workforce. Millennials are prepared to deal with the browning and graying of our society because it is all they have ever known. Since they grew up in schools and environments that were increasingly diverse, they are more likely to be in favor of diversity policies and acceptance.

This handbook is meant to help managers, employees, and anyone interested in a multigenerational workplace. The hope is that by highlighting and paying attention to another aspect of organizational diversity, organizations can reap benefits. Many believe that increased diversity in gender, race, status, and other areas has benefits to organization decisions and other outcomes. Adding generations to the diversity existing groups should provide organizations with increased benefits is managed correctly. Increasing employees' and managers' awareness and understanding of the differences can help combat potential challenges.

POINTS TO REMEMBER

- Do not profile based on generation. Such profiles are generalizations, and it is important not to stereotype people based on the profiles discussed in this book. Treat profiles like zodiac signs—all Virgos are not going to fit the traditional profile.
- Be open to honest conversation in the workplace. The only way to truly understand generational diversity is to create an environment that is open to communication and honesty. People should feel safe to share and have a culture of understanding differences.
- Consider generational differences as a value instead of a problem. Diversity of all kinds should be a value added to the organization and not a point of contention. Using the positive traits of each generation can increase organization efficiency and productivity. As discussed in chapter 3 on volunteering, Millennials and Baby Boomers share unique bonds that can make them great partners for work or school projects. Organizations should be aware of this when creating group or team assignments.
- Standardize orientation. Everyone in the organization should have a general understanding of professional norms and expectations held within the organization.
- Take turnover seriously. Retaining valued employees should be an important focus of any organization. Ensuring smooth leadership transitions with esteemed internal employees can only happen if you are able to keep these workers happy in their employment.
- Provide job counseling and job training. Workers of all ages want to know where they fit into the long-term vision of the organization. Showing employees that they have a future with the company and that they are valued is important to people in each generational cohort. The challenge is finding out the best way to demonstrate this for each generation. Some groups want you to "show them the money," while others may be happy with a simple "thank you."

References

*Achieve and Johnson, Grossnickle and Associates. 2013. *The Millennial Impact Report 2012.* Indianapolis: Achieve. http://cdn.trustedpartner.com/docs/library/AchieveMCON2013/TheMillennial ImpactReport2012.pdf (accessed January 22, 2014).

*Adams, S.J. 2000. Generation X: How Understanding This Population Leads to Better Safety Programs. *Professional Safety* 45(1), 26–29.

*Alonso, P., and G.B. Lewis. 2001. Public Service Motivation and Job Performance: Evidence from the Federal Sector. *American Review of Public Administration* 31(4), 363–380.

*Anderson, M.W. 2004. The Metrics of Workforce Planning. *Public Personnel Management* 33(4), 363–378.

*Arthur, J.B. 1994. Effects of Human Resource Systems on Manufacturing Performance and Turnover. *Academy of Management Journal* 37(3), 670–687.

*Bailey, D.E. and N.B. Kurland. 2002. A Review of Telework Research: Findings, New Directions, and Lessons for the Study of Modern Work. *Journal of Organizational Behavior,* (23) 383–400.

*Barak, M.E., J.A. Nissly, and A. Levin. 2001. Antecedents to Retention and Turnover Among Child Welfare, Social Work, and Other Human Service Employees: What Can We Learn From Past Research? A Review and Metanalysis. *Social Service Review* 75(4), 625–661.

*Baranyi, E.E. 2011. Volunteerism and Charitable Giving Among the Millennial Generation: How to Attract and Retain Millennials. Dissertations, Theses and Capstone Projects. Paper 451.

*Barnes, N.G. 2010a. Social Media Usage by Business, Higher Ed and Not for Profits. PowerPoint presentation. *Society for New Communications Research*, November 4–5. http://sncr.org/sites/default/files/Nora_Barnes_SNCR_Presentation_Social_Media_Usage.pdf.

*———. 2010b. *Social Media Usage Now Ubiquitous Among US Top Charities, Ahead of All Other Sectors.* University of Massachusetts, Dartmouth. www.umassd.edu/media/umassdartmouth/cmr/studiesandresearch/charity2010.pdf (accessed February 26, 2014).

*Bauerlein, M. 2009. Why Gen-Y Johnny Can't Read Nonverbal Cues. *Wall Street Journal*, September 4.

*Bechet, T.P. 2000. Developing Staffing Strategies That Work: Implementing Pragmatic, Nontraditional Approaches. *Public Personnel Management* 29(4), 465–476.

*Becker, G.S. 1962. Investment in Human Capital: A Theoretical Analysis. *Journal of Political Economy* 70(5), 9–49.

*Bertelli, A. 2007. Bureaucratic Turnover and Democratic Governance: Evidence from the U.S. Internal Revenue Service. *Journal of Public Administration Research and Theory* 17(2), 235–258.

*Bess, J.L. 1973. Integrating Faculty and Student Life Cycles. *Review of Educational Research* 43(4), 377–403.

*Bhagat, V., P. Loeb, and M. Rovner. 2010. *The Next Generation of American Giving: A Study on the Contrasting Charitable Habits of Generation Y, Generation X, Baby Boomers and Matures.* Arlington, VA: Edge Research. www.edgeresearch.com/Edge%20Research%20Case%20Study%20-%20 Next-Gen-Whitepaper.pdf (accessed January 21, 2014).

*Black, M., R. Moffitt, and J.T. Warner. 1990. The Dynamics of Job Separation: The Case of Federal Employees. *Journal of Applied Econometrics* 5(3), 245–262.

*Blackburn, R.T., and J.H. Lawrence. 1986. Aging and the Quality of Faculty Job Performance. *Review of Educational Research* 56(3), 265–290.

*Blau, F.D., and L.M. Kahn. 1981. Race and Sex Differences in Quits by Young Workers. *Industrial and Labor Relations Review* 34(4), 563–577.

*Bloom, J.R., J.A. Alexander, and B.A. Nichols. 1992. The Effect of the Social Organization of Work on the Voluntary Turnover Rate of Hospital Nurses in the United States. *Social Science Medicine* 34(12), 1413–1424.

*Boardman, P., B. Bozeman, and B. Ponomariov. 2010. Private Sector Imprinting: An Examination of the Impacts of Private Sector Job Experience on Public Manager's Work Attitudes. *Public Administration Review* 70(1), 50–59.

*Boath, D., and D.Y. Smith. 2004. When Your Best People Leave, Will Their Knowledge Leave, Too? *Harvard Management Update* (September), 6–7.

*Boeker, W., and J. Goodstein. 1993. Performance and Successor Choice: The Moderating Effects of Governance and Ownership. *Academy of Management Journal* (36)1, 172–186.

*Booth, A.L., M. Francesconi, and C. Garcia-Serrano. 1999. Job Tenure and Job Mobility. *Industrial and Labor Relations Review* 53(1), 43–70.

*Bowen, R.B. 2000. *Recognizing and Rewarding Employees.* New York: McGraw-Hill.

*Bozeman, B., and M.K. Feeney. 2009. Public Management Mentoring: What Affects Outcomes? *Journal of Public Administration Research and Theory* 19(2), 427–452.

*Bozeman, B., and B. Ponomariov. 2009. Sector Switching from a Business to a Government Job: Fast-Track Career or Fast Track to Nowhere? *Public Administration Review* 69(1), 77–91.

*Bradford, F.W. 1993. Understanding "Generation X." *Marketing Research* 5, 54.

*Brady, G.F., and D.L. Helmich. 1984. *Executive Succession.* Englewood Cliffs, NJ: Prentice-Hall.

*Brewer, G.A. 2002. Public Service Motivation: Theory, Evidence, and Prospects for Research. Paper presented at the Annual Meeting of the American Political Science Association, Boston, MA, p. 1.

*———. 2003. Building Social Capital: Civic Attitudes and Behavior of Public Servants. *Journal of Public Administration Research and Theory* 13(1), 5–26.

*Brewer, G.A., and S.C. Selden. 1998. Whistleblowers in the Federal Civil Service: New Evidence of the Public Service Ethic. *Journal of Public Administration Research and Theory* 8(3), 413–439.

*———. 2000. Why Elephants Gallop: Assessing and Predicting Organizational Performance in Federal Agencies. *Journal of Public Administration Research and Theory* 10(4), 685–711.

*Brewer, G.A., S.C. Selden, and R. Facer. 2000. Individual Conceptions of Public Service Motivation. *Public Administration Review* 60(3), 254–264.

*Buchanan, B. 1974. Government Managers, Business Executives, and Organizational Commitment. *Public Administration Review* 34 (July/August), 339–347.

*———. 1975. Red Tape and The Service Ethic: Some Unexpected Differences Between Public and Private Managers. *Administration & Society* 6 (February), 423–438.

*Callanan, G.A., and J.H. Greenhaus. 2008. The Baby Boom Generation and Career Management: A Call to Action. *Advances in Developing Human Resources* 10(1), 70–85

*Cannella, A.A. Jr., and M. Lubatkin. 1993. Succession As a Sociopolitical Process: Internal Impediments to Outsider Selection. *The Academy of Management Journal* 36(4), 763–793.

*Carrizales, T., and L. Bennett. 2013. A Public Service Education: A Review of Undergraduate Programs with a Community and Service Focus. *Journal of Public Affairs Education* 19(2), 309–323.

*Carroll, G.R. 1984. Dynamics of Publisher Succession in Newspaper Organizations. *Administrative Science Quarterly* 29, 93–133.

*Carroll, J.B., and Moss, D.A. 2002. State Employee Worker Shortage: The Impending Crisis. Lexington, KY: Council of State Governments.

*Catalyst. 2005. Exploding Generation X Myths: What the Next Batch of Leaders Want in Their Work/Personal Lives. *Journal of Accountancy* (August). www.journalofaccountancy.com/Issues/2005/Aug/ExplodingGenerationXMyths (Accessed January 5, 2009).

*Center on Philanthropy at Indiana University. 2008. *Generational Differences In Charitable Giving And In Motivations For Giving.* A report prepared for Campbell & Company. Indianapolis, IN: Indiana University, May.

*Cogitamus. 2012. *Current Use, Future Trends, and Opportunities in Public Sector Social Media.* NHS Federation, August. www.nhsconfed.org/Documents/cogitamus_report_Aug2012.pdf (accessed February 26, 2014).

*Collins, P.H. 2000. Gender, Black Feminism, and Black Political Economy. *The Annals of the American Academy of Political and Social Science* 568(1), 41–53.

*Colorado Nonprofit Association. N.d. "Talent Development Initiative: Path with a Heart." Colorado Nonprofit Association and Pathfinders Solutions. Accessed December 3, 2013. www.colorado nonprofits.org/training-events/talent-development-initiative/.

*Cone Inc. and AMP Agency. 2006. *The 2006 Cone Millennial Cause Study—The Millennial Generation: Pro-Social and Empowered to Change the World.* Boston: Cone Communications. www. prnewsonline.com/Assets/File/ConeMillennialCauseStudy_2006.pdf (accessed January 22, 2014).

*Cook Ross, Inc. 2004. Managing a Multigenerational Workforce. The Diversity Toolkit. Silver Spring, MD: Cook Ross, Inc.

*Cook, T.D. 1993. A Quasi-sampling Theory of the Generalization of Causal Relationships. *New Directions for Program Evaluation* 1993(57), 39–82.

*Cook, T.D., and D.T. Campbell. 1979. *Quasi-Experimentation: Design and Analysis Issues for Field Settings.* Chicago, IL: Rand McNally College Publishing.

*Cotton, J.L., and J.M. Tuttle. 1986. Employee Turnover: a Meta-analysis and Review with Implications for Research. *The Academy of Management Review* 11(1), 55–70.

*Crampton, S.M., and Hodge, J.W. 2006. The Supervisor and Generational Differences. Proceedings of the Academy of Organizational Culture, *Communications and Conflict*, 11. 19–22.

*Crewson, P.E. 1997. Public-Service Motivation: Building Empirical Evidence of Incidence and Effect. *Journal of Public Administration Research and Theory* 7(4), 499–518.

*Crosnoe, R., and G.H. Elder Jr. 2002. Successful Adaptation in the Later Years: a Life Course Approach to Aging. *Social Psychology Quarterly* 65(4), 309–328.

*Deal, Jennifer J. 2007. *Retiring the Generation Gap: How Employees Young and Old Can Find Common Ground.* San Francisco: Jossey-Bass.

*Dose, J.J. 1997. Work Values: An Integrative Framework and Illustrative Application to Organizational Socialization. *Journal of Occupational and Organizational Psychology* 70(3), 219–240.

*DoSomething.org. n.d.(a). Who We Are. http://217989-www5.dosomething.org/about/who-we-are.

*———. n.db. Young People and Volunteering. www.dosomething.org/blog/teens-and-volunteering.

*Downs, A. 1967. *Inside the Bureaucracy.* Santa Monica: RAND.

*Durst, S. 1999. The Effect of Family-friendly Programs on Public Organizations. *Review of Public Personnel Administration* 19(3), 19–33.

*Elder, G.H. 1998. Life Course and Human Development. In *Handbook of Child Psychology* (5th ed.), ed. William Damon, 939–991. New York: Wiley.

*Elder, G.H., and M.K. Johnson. 2002. The Life Course and Human Development: Challenges, Lessons, and New Directions. In *Invitation to the Life Course: Toward New Understandings of Later Life,* ed. Richard A. Settersten Jr.. Amityville, NY: Baywood.

*Elmore, T. 2012. In Other Words: Learning the Art of Communicating with the Next Generation. *Growing Leaders,* January 6. http://growingleaders.com/blog/in-other-words/ (accessed January 20, 2014).

*Erickson, R., J. Schwartz, and J. Ensell. 2012. The Talent Paradox: Critical Skills, Recession and the Illusion of Plenitude. *Deloitte Review* 2012(10), 78–91.

*Erikson, E.H. 1980. *Identity and the Life Cycle.* New York: W.W. Norton.

*Fagan, R., J. Pryor, and A. Mitchell. 2012. Talent Development Initiative. *Colorado Nonprofit Association.* www.coloradononprofits.org/training-events/talent-development-initiative/ (accessed December 3, 2013).

*Faith, R.L., R.S. Higgins, and R.D. Tollison. 1984. Managerial Rents and Outside Recruitment in the Coasian Firm. *American Economic Review* 74, 660–672.

*Falco, Tish. 2011. *Taking Social Media Public: Social Media for Successful Citizen Relationship Management*. Somers, NY: IBM Global Business Services, October. www-935.ibm.com/services/us/en/attachments/pdf/Social_Media—RN_White_Paper.pdf (accessed February 26, 2014).

*Farber, H.S. 1998. Are Lifetime Jobs Disappearing? Job Duration in the United States, 1973–1993. In *Labor Statistics Measurement Issues,* ed. J. Haltiwanger, M. Manser, and R. Topel, 157–203. Chicago: University of Chicago Press.

*Fine, A. 2008. It's Time to Focus on a New Generation. *Chronicle of Philanthropy* 20(21), 22–22.

*Frank, S.A., and G.B. Lewis. 2004. Government Employees: Working Hard or Hardly Working? *American Review of Public Administration* 34(1), 36–51.

*Friedman, S.D., and H. Singh. 1989. CEO Succession Events and Stockholder Reaction: the Influence of Context and Event Context. *Academy of Management Journal* 32, 718–744

*Gibson, D.E. 2003. Developing the Professional Self-concept: Role Model Constructs in Early, Middle, and Late Career Stages. *Organization Science* 14(5), 591–610.

*Goodstein, J., and B. Warren. 1991. Turbulence at the Top: A New Perspective on Governance Structure Changes and Strategic Change. *Academy of Management Journal* (34)2, 306–330.

*Gothard, S., and M.J. Austin. 2010. *Leadership Succession Planning: Implications for Nonprofit Human Service Organizations.* Berkeley: Mack Center on Nonprofit Management in the Human Services, University of California, Berkeley, March. http://mackcenter.berkeley.edu/assets/files/articles/Leadership%20Succession%20Planning%20Implications%20for%20nonprofit%20Human%20Service%20Organizations.pdf (accessed January 5, 2013).

*Government Performance Project. 1998. *State Government Survey of Human Resource Management.* Syracuse, NY: Campbell Institute of Public Affairs.

*Gray, A.M., and V.I. Phillips. 1994. Turnover, Age and Length of Service: A Comparison of Nurses and Other Staff in the National Health Service. *Journal of Advanced Nursing* 19, 819–27.

*Groot, W., and M. Verberne. 1997. Aging, Job Mobility, and Compensation. *Oxford Economic Papers* 49(3), 380–403.

*Grusky, O. 1961. Corporate Size, Bureaucratization, and Managerial Succession. *The American Journal of Sociology* 67(3), 261–269.

*Hall, R.E. 1982. The Importance of Lifetime Jobs in the U.S. Economy. *American Economic Review* 72(4), 716–724.

*Hammill, Greg. 2005. Mixing and Managing Four Generations of Employees. *FDU Magazine Online* (winter/spring). www.fdu.edu/newspubs/magazine/05ws/generations.htm (accessed November 23, 2013).

*Hicks, R., and K. Hicks. 1999. *Boomers, Xers, and other Strangers: Understanding the Generational Differences that Divide Us.* Wheaton, IL: Tyndale House.

*Hirsh, B.T., and D.A. Macpherson. 2003. Union Membership and Coverage Database from the Current Population Survey: Note. *Industrial and Labor Relations Review* 56(2), 349–354.

*Houlihan, Anne. 2008. When Gen-X is in Charge: How to Harness the Younger Leadership Style. *Security* 45(4), 42–43.

*Houston, D.J. 2000. Public Service Motivation: A Multivariate Test. *Journal of Public Administration Research and Theory* 10(4), 713–727.

*———. 2006. "Walking the Walk of Public Service Motivation": Public Employees and Charitable Gifts of Time, Blood, and Money. *Journal of Public Administration Research and Theory* 16(1), 67–86.

*Howe, N., and W. Strauss. 2000. *Millennials Rising: The Next Great Generation.* New York: Vintage.

*iGov Survey. 2013. *The Use of Social Media in the Public Sector Survey 2013.* Survey. www.igovsurvey.com/surveys/view/21 (accessed February 26, 2014)

*Illinois Civil Service Commission. 2009. *Annual Report for Fiscal Year 2009.* Springfield, IL, October.

*Ippolito, R.A. 1987. Why Federal Workers Don't Quit. *The Journal of Human Resources* 22(2), 281–299.

*Ito, J.K. 2003. Career Branding and Mobility in the Civil Service: An Empirical Study. *Public Personnel Management* 32(2), 1–21.

*Jarousse, L.A. 2011. Best Practices for Recruitment & Retention. *H&HN*, April 1. www.hhnmag.com/hhnmag/jsp/articledisplay.jsp?dcrpath=HHNMAG/Article/data/04APR2011/0411HHN_FEA_gatefold&domain=HHNMAG (accessed December 3, 2013).

*Jenkins, J. 2014. Leading the Four Generations at Work. *American Management Association.* http://www.amanet.org/training/articles/Leading-the-Four-Generations-at-Work.aspx (accessed February 10, 2015)

*Jenkins, R. 2013. Are You Making this Classic Leadership Mistake When Leading Millennials? *Ryan-Jenkins.com,* September 30. http://ryan-jenkins.com/2013/09/30/are-you-making-this-classic-leadership-mistake-when-leading-millennials/ (accessed January 20, 2014).

*Jennings AT. 2000. Hiring Generation-X. *Journal of Accountancy* 189, 55–59

*Johnson, G.L., and J. Brown. 2004. Workforce Planning Not a Common Practice, IPMA-HR study finds. *Public Personnel Management* 33(4), 379–388.

*Johnson, M.K. 2001. Job Values in the Young Adult Transition: Change and Stability with Age. *Social Psychology Quarterly* 64(4), 297–317.

*Jorgenson, B. 2003. Baby Boomers, Generation X and Generation Y: Policy Implications for Defense Forces in the Modern Era. *Foresight,* 5, 41–49.

*Joyner, T. 2000. Gen X-ers Focus on Life outside the Job Fulfillment. *The Secured Lender* 56(3), 64–68.

*Judge, T.A., and R.D. Bretz. 1994. Political Influence Behavior and Career Success. *Journal of Management* 20(1), 43–65.

*Jurkiewicz, C.E. 2000. Generation X and the Public Employee. *Public Personnel Management,* 29, 55–74.

*Jurkiewicz, C.E., and R.C. Brown. 1998. GenXers vs. Boomers vs. Matures: Generational Comparisons of Public Employee Motivation. *Review of Public Personnel Administration* 18, 18–37.

*Karl, K.A., and B. Peat. 2004. A Match Made in Heaven or a Square Peg in a Round Hole? How Public Service Educators Can Help Students Assess Person-environment Fit. *Journal of Public Affairs Education* 10(4), 265–277.

*Karp, H., Fuller, C., and D. Sirias. 2002. Bridging the Boomer Xer Gap. Creating Authentic Teams for High Performance at Work. Palo Alto, CA: Davies-Black Publishing.

*Karp, H., D. Sirias, and K. Arnold. 1999. Teams: Why Generation X Marks the Spot. *The Journal for Quality and Participation* 22(4), 30–33.

*Katzell, M.E. 1968. Expectations and Dropouts in Schools of Nursing. *Journal of Applied Psychology* 52(2), 154–157.

*Kellough, J.E. and W. Osuna. 1995. Cross-agency Comparisons of Quit Rates in the Federal Service: Another Look at the Evidence. *Review of Public Personnel Administration* 15(4), 15–68.

*Kerrigan, H. 2011. Fighting to Save the MPA. *Governing* (August). www.governing.com/topics/public-workforce/fighting-save-MPA.html (accessed January 15, 2014).

*Kersten, D. 2002. Today's Generations Face New Communication Gaps. *USA Today,* November 15. http://usatoday30.usatoday.com/money/jobcenter/workplace/communication/2002-11-15-communication-gap_x.htm (accessed April 15, 2008)

*Kim, S. 2005. Factors Affecting State Government Information Technology Turnover Intentions. *American Review of Public Administration* 35(2), 137–156.

*Kingsley, C. 2010. Making the Most of Social Media: 7 Lessons from Successful Cities. Philadelphia, PA: Fels Institute of Government, March 9. www.fels.upenn.edu/sites/www.fels.upenn.edu/files/PP3_SocialMedia.pdf.

*Ko, K., and L. Han. 2013. An Empirical Study on Public Service Motivation of the Next Generation Civil Servants in China. *Public Personnel Management* 42(2), 191–222.

*Kohn, M., and C. Schooler. 1983. *Work and Personality: An Inquiry into the Impact of Social Stratification.* Norwood, NJ: Ablex.

*Kopfer, D. L. 2004. Workplace Attitudes of Generation X. M.A. Thesis.

*Kupperschmidt, B. 2000. Multigeneration Employees: Strategies for Effective Management. *Health Care Manager* 19(1), 65–76.

*Lancaster, L. C., and D. Stillman. 2002. *When Generations Collide.* New York: HarperCollins.

*Lavigna, B., and J. Flato. 2014. Millennials Are Attracted to Public Service, but Government Needs to Deliver. *ERE.net*, January 22. www.ere.net/2014/01/22/millennials-are-attracted-to-public-service-but-government-needs-to-deliver/.

*Laz, C. 1998. Act Your Age. *Sociological Forum* 13(1), 85–113.

*Lazear, E. P. 1999. Personnel Economics: Past Lessons and Future Directions. *Journal of Labor Economics* 17(2), 199–236.

*Lechman, K. N.d. "Communicating Across Generations." Columbus, OH: The Ohio State University Extension. http://extensionhr.osu.edu/profdev/Microsoft%20PowerPoint%20-%20Communicating%20Across%20Generations%20Presentation%20for%20Web%20Ex%20May%2013,%202010%20Power%20Point.pdf. (accessed January 20, 2014.)

*Lee, S., and A. B. Whitford. 2008. Exit, Voice, Loyalty and Pay: Evidence from the Public Workforce. *Journal of Public Administration Research and Theory* 18(4), 647–671.

*Leibowitz, J. 2004. Bridging the Knowledge and Skills Gap: Tapping Federal Retirees. *Public Personnel Management* 33(4), 421–448.

*Lenhart, A., K. Purcell, A. Smith, and K. Zickuhr. 2010. Social Media and Young Adults. *Pew Research Internet Project,* February 3. www.pewinternet.org/2010/02/03/social-media-and-young-adults/.

*Leonhardt, D. 2013. The Idled Young Americans. *The New York Times,* May 3. www.nytimes.com/2013/05/05/sunday-review/the-idled-young-americans.html?pagewanted=all.

*Lewis, G. B. 1991. Turnover and the Quiet Crisis in the Federal Government. *Public Administration Review* 51(2), 145–155.

*Lewis, G. B., and M. Ha. 1988. Impact of the Baby Boom on Career Success in Federal Civil Service. *Public Administration Review* 48(6), 951–956.

*Lewis, G. B., and K. Park. 1989. Turnover Rates in the Federal Civil Service. *American Review of Public Administration* 18(1), 13–28.

*Liberto, J. 2013. Wave of Federal Retirees to Hit Government. *CNN Money,* June 13. http://money.cnn.com/2013/06/13/news/federal-workers-retire/.

*Lindsay, P., and W. E. Knox. 1984. Continuity and Change in Work Values Among Young Adults. *American Journal of Sociology* 89(4), 918–931.

*Losey, Stephen. 2013. Leaders Fear Sequester's Impact on Recruitment, Retention, Service. *Federal Times,* May 6.

*Manning, C. 2014. "Communicating with the Millennial Generation." Presentation. www.cdph.ca.gov/programs/wicworks/Documents/Millennial%20Generation/WIConnects%20Presentations/Communicating%20with%20the%20Millennial%20Generation.pdf. (accessed January 20, 2014.)

*March, J. G., and H. A. Simon. 1958. *Organizations.* New York: Wiley.

*Marston, C. 2007. *Motivating the "What's in It for Me" Workforce: Manage Across the Generational Divide and Increase Profits.* Hoboken, NJ: John Wiley & Sons.

*Mathews, A. 1998. Diversity: A Principle of Human Resource Management. *Public Personnel Management* 27(2), 175–186.

*Meier, K. J., and A. Hicklin. 2008. Employee Turnover and Organizational Performance: A Theoretical Extension and Test with Public Sector Data. *Journal of Public Administration Research and Theory* 18(4), 573–590.

*Mergel, I. 2010. Government 2.0 Revisited: Social Media Strategies in the Public Sector. *PA Times* 33(3), 7, 10.

*MetLife. 2013. *A Demographic Profile: America's Gen X.* Mature Market Institute Publication MMI 00128(0210). www.metlife.com/assets/cao/mmi/publications/Profiles/mmi-gen-x-demographic-profile.pdf (accessed February 2, 2013).

*Miller, D. 1991. Stale in the Saddle: CEO Tenure and the Match Between Organization and Environment. *Management Science* 37(1), 34–52.

*Miniter, R. 1997. Generation X Does Business. *The American Enterprise* 8(4), 38–40.

*Mishel, L., J. Bernstein, and J. Schmitt. 2001. *The State of Working America, 2000/2001.* Ithaca, NY: Cornell University Press.

*Mitchell, S. 2000. *American Generations: Who They Are, How They Live, What They Think.* 3d ed. Ithaca, NY: New Strategist Publications.

*Mobley, W. H. 1977. Intermediate Linkages in the Relationship Between Job Satisfaction and Employee Turnover. *Journal of Applied Psychology* 62(2), 237–240.

*———. 1982. Some Unanswered Questions in Turnover and Withdrawal Research. *The Academy of Management Review* 7(1), 111–116.

*Mobley, W. H., R. W. Griffeth, H. H. Hand, and B. M. Meglino. 1979. Review and Conceptual Analysis of the Employee Turnover Process. *Psychological Bulletin* 86(3), 493–522.

*Mortimer, J. T., and J. Lorence. 1979. Work and Experience and Occupational Value Socialization: A Longitudinal Study. *American Journal of Sociology* 84(6), 1361–1385.

*Moynihan, D. P., and N. Landuyt. 2008. Explaining Turnover Intention in State Government: Examining the Roles of Gender, Life Cycle, and Loyalty. *Review of Public Personnel Administration* 28(2), 120–143.

*Moynihan, D. P., and S. J. Pandey. 2007. The Role of Organizations in Fostering Public Service Motivation. *Public Administration Review* 67(1), 40–53.

*———. 2008. The Ties that Bind: Social Networks, Person-organization Value Fit, and Turnover Intention. *Journal of Public Administration Research and Theory* 18(2), 205–227.

*Muchinsky, P. M., and P. C. Morrow. 1980. A Multidisciplinary Model of Voluntary Employee Turnover. *Journal of Vocational Behavior* 17(3), 263–290.

*National Commission on the Public Service. 2003. *Urgent Business: Revitalizing the Federal Government for the 21st Century.* Washington, DC: The National Commission on the Public Service, January.

*National Conference on Citizenship. N.d. Two Special Generations: The Millennials and the Boomers. http://ncoc.net/226.

*Nigro, L. G., and F. A. Nigro. 2000. *The New Public Personnel Administration.* 5th ed. Itasca, IL: F.E. Peacock.

*Nilles, Jack M. 1975. Telecommunications and Organizational Decentralization. *IEEE Transactions on Communications* 23(10), 1142–1147.

*Nonprofit Technology Network (NTEN), Common Knowledge, and Blackbaud. 2012. *4th Annual Nonprofit Social Network Benchmark Report 2012.* www.oregonnonprofitleadersconference.org/wp-content/uploads/2012/12/2012-Nonprofit-Social-Networking-Benchmark-Report.pdf (accessed February 26, 2014).

*O'Bannon, G. 2001. Managing Our Future: The Generation X Factor. *Public Personnel Management* 30, 95–109.

*O'Rand, A. M., and M. L. Krecker. 1990. Concepts of the Life Cycle: Their History, Meanings, and Uses in the Social Sciences. *Annual Review of Sociology* 16, 214–262.

*Parker, V. A. 2002. Connecting Relational Work and Workgroup Context in Caregiving Organizations. *Journal of Applied Behavioral Science,* 38(3), 276–97.

*Partnership for Public Service. 2005. Federal Brain Drain. Issue Brief PPS-05–08, November 21.

*Perry, J. L. 1996. Measuring Public Service Motivation: An Assessment of Construct Reliability and Validity. *Journal of Public Administration Research and Theory* 6(1), 5–22.

*———. 1997. Antecedents of Public Service Motivation. *Journal of Public Administration Research and Theory* 7(2), 181–197.

*———. 2000. Bringing Society In: Toward a Theory of Public-service Motivation. *Journal of Public Administration Research and Theory* 10(2), 471–488.

*Perry, J. L., and L. R. Wise. 1990. The Motivational Bases of Public Service. *Public Administration Review* 50(3), 367–373.

*Pettman, B. O. 1975. External and Personal Determinants of Labour Turnover. In *Labour Turnover and Retention,* ed. B. O. Pettman, 31–50. Epping: Gower Press.

*Porter, L. W., and R. W. Steers. 1973. Organizational, Work, and Personal Factors in Employee Turnover and Absenteeism. *Psychological Bulletin* 80(2), 151–176.

*Preston, C. 2010. When it Comes to Appeals, Charities Need to Work on Filling the Generation Gap, a New Study Finds. *Chronicle of Philanthropy* 22(9), 6–6.

*Price, J. L. 1975. A Theory of Turnover. In *Labour Turnover and Retention,* ed. B. O. Pettman, 51–75. Epping: Gower Press.

*———. 1976. The Effects of Turnover on the Organization. *Organization and Administrative Sciences* 7, 61–88.

*———. 1977. *The Study of Turnover.* Ames: Iowa State University Press.

*Pynes, J. E. 2002. Strategic Human Resource Management. In *Public Personnel Administration: Problems and Prospects* (4th ed.), ed. Steven W. Hays and Richard C. Kearney, 93–105. Uppers Saddle River, NJ: Prentice Hall.

*Rainey, H. 1982. Reward Preferences Among Public and Private Managers: In Search of the Service Ethic. *American Review of Public Administration* 16(4), 288–302.

*Randstad Work Solutions. 2007. World of Work Survey. http://us.randstad.com/content/aboutrandstad/knowledge-center/employer-resources/World-of-Work-2008.pdf (accessed February 1, 2015).

*Reingold, D., and R. Nesbit. 2006. *Volunteer Growth in America: A Review of Trends Since 1974.* Washington, DC: Corporation for National & Community Service, December. www.nationalservice.gov/pdf/06_1203_volunteer_growth.pdf (accessed January 22, 2014).

*Rhodes, S. R. 1983. Age-related Differences in Work Attitudes and Behavior: A Review and Conceptual Analysis. *Psychological Bulletin*, 93, 328–367.

*Rikleen, L. S. 2011. *Creating Tomorrow's Leaders: the Expanding Roles of Millennials in the Workplace.* Executive Briefing Series. Chestnut Hill, MA: Boston College Center for Work & Family, September 12. www.bc.edu/content/dam/files/centers/cwf/pdf/BCCWF%20EBS-Millennials%20FINAL.pdf (accessed January 21, 2014).

*Robinson, S. L. and E. W. Morrison. 2000. The Development of Psychological Contract Breach and Violation: A Longitudinal Study. *Journal of Organizational Behavior*, 21(5), 525–546.

*Ross, I. C., and A. Zander. 1957. Need Satisfactions and Employee Turnover. *Personnel Psychology* 10(3), 327–338.

*Ryan, M. 2000. Gerald Celente: He Reveals What Lies Ahead. *Parade Magazine,* September 10, 22–23.

*Sanders, R. M. 2004. GeorgiaGain or GeorgiaLoss? The Great Experiment in State Civil Service Reform. *Public Personnel Management* 33(2), 151–164.

*Scanlon, Janet, and Marcie Pitt-Catsouphes. 2005. Generations X and Work/life Values: An Interview with Paulette Gerkovich. *The Network News* 7(2).

*Schaie, K. W. 1965. A General Model for the Study of Developmental Problems. *Psychological Bulletin* 64(2), 92–107.

*Scott, L. 2004. Trends in State Personnel Administration. In *The Book of the States* 36, 401–404. Lexington, KY: The Council of State Governments.

*Selden, S. C., and D. P. Moynihan. 2000. A Model of Voluntary Turnover in State Government. *Review of Public Personnel Administration* 20(2), 63–74.

*Shelton, C., and L. Shelton. 2005. *The NeXt Revolution: What Gen X Women Want at Work and How Their Boomer Bosses Can Help Them to Get It.* Mountain View, CA: Davies-Black.

*Singer Group, Inc. 1999. *Arrival of Generation X in the Workforce: Implications for Compensation and Benefits.* Annual Benefits and Compensation Update WEB Baltimore Chapter.

*Singer, H. A., and P. R. Abramson. 1973. Values of Business Administrators: A Longitudinal Study. *Psychological Reports* 33(1), 43–46.

*Skytland, N. 2011. 7 Tips to Effectively Communicate with the Next Generation. *open.NASA,* December 4. http://open.nasa.gov/blog/2011/12/04/7-tips-to-effectively-communicate-with-the-next-generatio/ (accessed January 20, 2014).

*Smith, C. B. 1979. Influence of Internal Opportunity Structure and Sex of Worker on Turnover Patterns. *Administrative Science Quarterly* 24(3), 362–381.

*Smith, G.P. 2007. Baby Boomer Versus Generation X: Managing the New Workforce. Chart Your Course International. http://www.chartcourse.com/comments-about-generation-x-and-baby-boomers/ (accessed February 10, 2015).

*Smith, H.L. 2008. Advances in Age Period Cohort Analysis. *Sociological Methods Research* 36(3), 287–296.

*Smola, K.W., and C.D. Sutton. 2002. Generational Differences: Revisiting Generational Work Values for the New Millennium. *Journal of Organizational Behavior* 23(4), 363–382.

*Somers, M.J. 1996. Modelling Employee Withdrawal Behavior Over Time: A Study of Turnover Using Survival Analysis. *Journal of Occupational and Organizational Psychology* 69(4), 315–326.

*State of Washington. 2000. *Workforce Planning Guide: Right People, Right Jobs, Right Time.* Olympia: State of Washington, Department of Personnel, December.

*Staw, B.M., and G.R. Oldham. 1978. Reconsidering Our Dependent Variables: A Critique and Empirical Study. *Academy of Management Journal* 21(4), 539–559.

*Steiner, G.A., and J.F. Steiner. 2000. *Business, Government, and Society: A Managerial Perspective.* 9th ed. New York: Irwin McGraw-Hill.

*Sullivan, J. 2002. Workforce: Why To Start Now. *Workforce* 81(12), 46–50.

*Sun, C. 2011. 10+ Ways to Minimize Generational Differences in the Workplace. *Tech Republic,* January 18. www.techrepublic.com/blog/10-things/10-plus-ways-to-minimize-generational-differences-in-the-workplace/ (accessed November 22, 2013).

*Taylor, P., and S. Keeter (eds.). 2010. *Millennials: A Portrait of Generation Next.* Washington, DC: Pew Research Center, February. www.pewsocialtrends.org/files/2010/10/millennials-confident-con-nected-open-to-change.pdf.

*Tharenou, P. 1999. Is There a Link Between Family Structures and Women's and Men's Managerial Career Advancement? *Journal of Organizational Behavior* 20(6), 837–863.

*The National Oceanographic and Atmospheric Association Office of Diversity. 2006. Tips to Improve the Interaction Among the Generations: Traditionalists, Boomers, X'ers and Nexters. Retrieved June 20, 2015 http://big.colostate.edu/mti/tips/pages/InteractionAmongTheGenerations.aspx

*The Yong Professionals for Covenant House. (n.d.). About the Young Professionals for Covenant House. Retrieved from http://www.youngpros.net/index.php/home.html.

*Tolbize, A. 2008. *Generation Differences in the Workplace.* Minneapolis: University of Minnesota, August 16.

*Topel, R.H., and M.P. Ward. 1992. Job Mobility and the Careers of Young Men. *The Quarterly Journal of Economics* 107(2), 439–479.

*Trimble, D.E. 2006. Organizational Commitment, Job Satisfaction, and Turnover Intention of Mission-aries. *Journal of Psychology and Theology* 34(4), 349–360.

*Tufts University. N.d. Tufts 1+4 Key Questions & Concepts. Jonathan M. Tisch College of Citizenship and Public Service. http://activecitizen.tufts.edu/tufts14/tufts-14-key-concepts/.

*Twenge, J.M., and S.M. Campbell. 2008. Generational Differences in Psychological Traits and Their Impact on the Workplace. *Journal of Managerial Psychology* 23(8), 862–877.

*Ureta, M. 1992. The Importance of Lifetime Jobs in the United States Economy, Revisited. *American Economic Review* 82(1), 322–335.

*U.S. Bureau of Labor Statistics. 2010. Projections Overview. In *Occupational Outlook Handbook Online.* www.bls.gov/ooh/about/print/projections-overview.htm (accessed December 19, 2013).

*U.S. General Services Administration. 2014. Social Media Initiatives at GSA. February 25. www.gsa.gov/socialmedia.

*U.S. Merit Systems Protection Board. 2008. *Attracting the Next Generation: A Look at Federal Entry-Level New Hires.* A Report to the President and the Congress of the United States, Washington, DC: U.S. Merit Systems Protection Board, January.

*U.S. Office of Government Ethics. 2010. Government Ethics and the Use of Social Media. The 18th National Government Ethics Conference, Chicago, Illinois, Wednesday, May 12. www.epa.gov/ogc/2010ethicstraining/Session%207%20Handout%20Gov%20Ethics%20and%20the%20Use%20of%20Social%20Media.pdf.

*USA.gov. N.d. Mobile apps gallery. http://apps.usa.gov/.

*Valenti, M.V. 2001. Generation X: Act Your Stage! Organizational Commitment and Career Stage Perspectives. PhD thesis, New York University, Graduate School of Arts and Science.

*Valueoptions.com. Generation Y [Born 1980–1994]. http://www.valueoptions.com/spotlight_YIW/gen_y.htm (Accessed February 1, 2015)

*Valueoptions.com. Generation X [Born 1965–1980]. http://www.valueoptions.com/spotlight_YIW/gen_x.htm (Accessed February 1, 2015)

*Valueoptions.com. The Baby Boomer Generation [Born 1946–1964]. http://www.valueoptions.com/spotlight_YIW/baby_boomers.htm (Accessed February 1, 2015).

*Walsh, B.D., T. Vacha-Hasse, and J.T. Kapes. 1996. The Values Scale: Differences Across Grade Levels for Ethnic Minority Students. *Educational and Psychological Measurement* 56(2), 263–276.

*Walsh, J.P., and J.K. Seward. 1990. On the Efficiency of Internal and External Corporate Control Mechanisms. *The Academy of Management Review* 15(3), 421–458.

*Weber, M. 1947. *The Theory of Social and Economic Organizations,* trans. A.M. Henderson and T. Parsons. New York: Free Press.

*Weitz, J. 1956. Job Expectancy and Survival. *Journal of Applied Psychology* 40, 245–247.

*West, J.P. 2002. Georgia On The Mind of Radical Civil Service Reformers. *Review of Public Personnel Administration* 22(2), 79–93.

*Wilson, J. 2000. Volunteering. *Annual Review Sociology* 26: 215–40

*Wittmer, D. 1991. Serving the People or Serving for Pay: Reward Preferences Among Government, Hybrid Sector, and Business Managers. *Public Productivity and Management Review* 14(4), 369 383.

*Wolf, J.F., C.M. Neves, R.T. Greenough, and B.B. Benton. 1987. Greying at the Temples: Demographics of a Public Service Occupation. *Public Administration Review* 47(2), 190–198.

*Yang, Y. and K.C. Land. 2008. Age Period Cohort Analysis of Repeated Cross-section Surveys: Fixed or Random Effects? *Sociological Methods Research* 36(3), 297–326.

*Young, Mary B. 2003. *The Aging-and-Retiring Government Workforce: How Serious Is the Challenge? What Are Jurisdictions Doing about It?* The Center for Organizational Research, http://www.accenture.com/SiteCollectionDocuments/PDF/CPS_AgeBubble_ExecutiveSummary.pdf (accessed February 10, 2015).

*Yu, Hc and Miller, P. 2005. Leadership style-The X Generation and Baby Boomers compared in different cultural contexts. *Leadership and Organization Management Journal* 26(1), pp. 35–50.

**Zemke, R., Raines, C., and Filipczak, B. 2000. *Generations At Work: Managing the Clash of Veterans, Boomers, Xers, and Nexters in Your Workplace.* New York: AMACOM.

About the Author

Madinah F. Hamidullah is an assistant professor and director of undergraduate programs in the School of Public Affairs and Administration at Rutgers University–Newark. Her current research interests include diversity, generational differences, and public service motivation. Dr. Hamidullah teaches in the Master of Public Administration program and the undergraduate program in Public and Nonprofit Administration. She teaches courses in public management, leadership, human resource management, and service learning. Dr. Hamidullah holds a bachelor of arts (in dance and political science) and master of public administration from the University of North Carolina at Charlotte. She received her PhD in public administration and policy from the University of Georgia.

Index

References to figures are shown in *italics* and references to tables are in **bold**.